Welcome

When I launched *Music Tech Magazine* in early 2003 there was a new version of Logic on the block: Emagic's Logic 6 had just been given its big launch at that year's Winter NAMM show – and it was kicking up a storm. Apple hadn't long bought Emagic and version 6 of Logic was the first one in some years that – controversially – wasn't available on the PC platform.

It wasn't long before Apple ditched the Emagic name and took Logic 'in house', applying its industry-beating ergonomics and design form to future versions of the software – the product has improved with each new release. Now Logic Pro 8 is part of the Logic Studio bundle, which offers users tremendous amounts of additional software and Apple Loops for a mere £329. This represents incredible value for money and is – in our opinion – reason enough on its own to buy an Apple Mac!

In this, the third in our series of *Music Tech Focus* magazines, we present you with over 20 Logic Pro Workshops and Walkthroughs, plus a (fascinating) history of Logic, a complete introduction to the software, the full review of Logic Studio from the *Music Tech* archives, as well as interviews with leading artists who use

This represents incredible value for money and is – in our opinion – reason enough to buy a Mac!

the package, our pick of the third-party plug-ins for Logic and, of course, the *Music Tech Focus* DVD, which contains Logic session and audio files for you to use with the Workshops, as well as plug-in demos and an incredible 1.5 hours of video tuition from our friends at macProVideo.

And, if you like this mag, don't forget that the Ableton Live and Reason Focus issues are still available for purchase – turn to page 120 to find out how to grab yourself a copy of these.

Paul Pettengale Editorial Director

MusicTech Focus

MUSIC TECH FOCUS
www.musictechmag.co.uk
Anthem Publishing Ltd
Suite 6, Piccadilly House
London Road,
Bath BA1 6PL
Tel +44 (0) 1225 489984
Fax +44 (0) 1225 489980
editorial@anthem-publishing.com

Editorial Director Paul Pettengale
paul.pettengale@anthem-publishing.com
Art Editor Kai Wood
kai.wood@anthem-publishing.com
Deputy Editor Lewis Brangwyn
lewis.brangwyn@anthem-publishing.com
Production Editor Jon Palmer
jon.palmer@anthem-publishing.com

Contributors
Mark Cousins, Mo Volans, Mike Hillier

Art Director Jenny Cook
jenny.cook@anthem-publishing.com
Advertising Director Simon Lewis
simon.lewis@anthem-publishing.com
Managing Director Jon Bickley
jon.bickley@anthem-publishing.com

Subscriptions to Music Tech Magazine
Tel +44 (0) 870 444 8468
Email subs@anthem-publishing.com
Price (12 issues) £71.88
UK basic annual rate

Printed by Benham Goodhead Print
Tel +44 (0) 1869 363333

Distributed by Marketforce (UK) Ltd,
The Blue Fin Building
110 Southwark Street
London SE1 0SU
Tel +44 (0) 20 3148 3300

Licensing enquiries Bruce Sawford
+44 (0) 1280 860185
Bruce@BruceSawfordLicensing.com

MusicTech Focus

Logic Pro
The in-depth guide for the creative musician

132 PAGES OF PURE LOGIC PRO!

62 PAGES OF LOGIC PRO WORKSHOPS

FEATURING...
- 16 Logic Pro 8 Workshops ▥ 6 Logic Pro 7 Workshops
- The best third-party plug-ins ▥ 5 pro user interviews
- The history of Logic Pro ▥ Logic controllers reviewed

Anthem

Written and compiled by Music Tech Magazine's Logic Pro experts

MUSIC TECH FOCUS LOGIC PRO

CONTENTS

132 PAGES OF PURE LOGIC PRO!

▶ ON YOUR MusicTech DVD ROM
Turn to page 130 to find out what's on this issue's MusicTech Focus DVD.

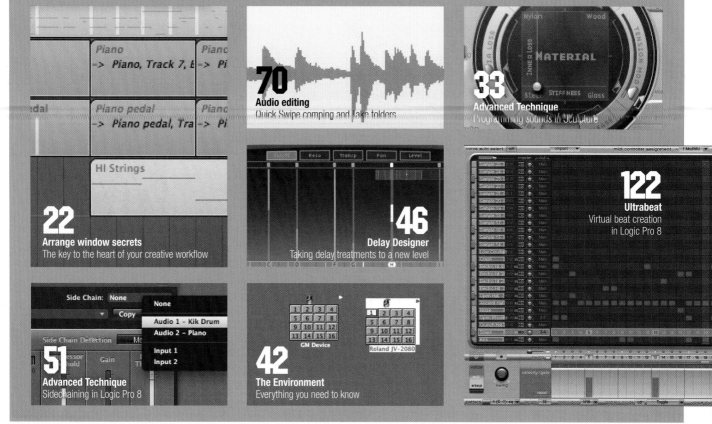

16 Logic Pro 8 workshops, including...

70
Audio editing
Quick Swipe comping and take folders

33
Advanced Technique
Programming sounds in Sculpture

22
Arrange window secrets
The key to the heart of your creative workflow

46
Delay Designer
Taking delay treatments to a new level

122
Ultrabeat
Virtual beat creation in Logic Pro 8

51
Advanced Technique
Sidechaining in Logic Pro 8

42
The Environment
Everything you need to know

6 Logic Pro 7 workshops, including…

116 Spectral Gate
Your door to a new range of sounds

exciter
26 SubBass and Exciter
The top and the bottom of it all

90 EXS24 data management
Improving efficiency and creativity

Reviews

10 Logic Studio
The low-down on version 8

79 Logic Pro monitors
Nearfield thinking

60 Logic Pro controllers
…to suit all budgets

Interviews

28 Stanton Warriors
The breakbeat duo
explain why they use Logic

37 Slam
Embracing technology
in the world of techno

118 Danny Byrd
One man's journey from
the Atari ST to Logic Pro

Feature
Expanding
Logic: our pick
of the best
third-party
plug-ins
96

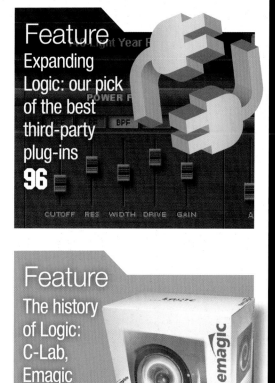

Feature
The history
of Logic:
C-Lab,
Emagic
and Apple
06

The history

From a MIDI sequencer on the Atari ST to one of Apple's leading creative applications, Logic has redefined music production, as **Mark Cousins** explains.

Being at the cutting edge of computer-based recording for almost 20 years is no mean feat, but Logic has witnessed it all – from the early days of MIDI sequencing, right through to today's hi-tech virtual studio. The history of Logic, therefore, offers a real insight into how the computer has revolutionised music production, transforming it from a niche activity for those who dared to connect together a roomful of expensive synthesizers with a MIDI cable to the point where anybody using GarageBand can have access to a complete digital multitrack production environment using nothing more than an off-the-shelf laptop!

The seeds of Logic date back to a German company called C-Lab and a music application they had developed in 1988 called Notator. In the late 80s, the world of computer-based music was led by the MIDI sequencer, using an Atari ST and applications like Cubase or Notator to control a rack of hardware samplers and synthesizers. Despite being one of the more expensive packages, Notator became a big hit for C-Lab and a major rival to the market-leading Cubase. Even at this point, components of today's Logic were clearly to be seen, including the Score Editor, Sequence parameters, List Editing and so on.

The birth of Emagic

In 1992 Gerhard Lengeling and Chris Adam, two of C-Lab's most prominent programmers, left to form Emagic, taking with them the code to the successor to the

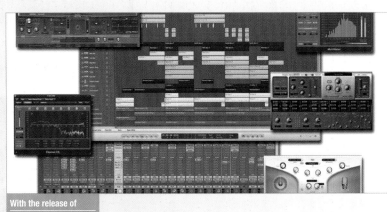

With the release of Logic Studio, Logic has grown up to become one of the most complete solutions for computer-based audio and music production.

Notator throne, Notator Logic. The concept behind Notator Logic (first released in 1993 for the Atari ST) was to create a completely flexible, customisable working environment; a sequencer that offered no restrictions to either your creative or technical workflow. Even more important to Notator Logic's user base, though, was the adoption of an object-orientated approach, pioneered by Cubase, where MIDI data could be recorded and edited as a series of graphic regions, rather than the rigid pattern-based approach of the original Notator.

Along with the birth of Notator Logic came the eventual demise of the Atari ST, with many users keen to take advantage of the increasing performance and usability of the Macintosh computer. Version 1.6 seamlessly ported Notator Logic – now retitled simply as Logic – to the Mac platform, which set the scene for the next chapter in Logic's development.

In the early 90s, as computing performance finally started to reach acceptable levels, the realistic possibility of handling audio production inside a computer started to emerge. The most notable system at this time was Digidesign's Pro Tools, which used an expensive ▶

> "The history of Logic offers a real insight into how the computer has revolutionised music production."

LOGIC TIMELINE

Notator Logic 1.5, 1993

■ Notator Logic set new standards for MIDI sequencing on the Atari ST and, later, the Apple Mac. It adopted Cubase's innovative object-orientated approach to music sequencing, augmenting this with lots of flexibility and customisability.

Logic Audio 2, 1995

■ Logic version 2 saw the application finally move over to the PC, joining the now well-established Mac version. The addition of audio functionality into a version called Logic Audio enabled users of Digidesign's Pro Tools hardware to experiment with hard disk recording on the Mac, using Logic as the front end.

# of Logic Pro

DEVELOPING LOGIC STUDIO
Apple's Xander Soren and Bill Hunt on the inspiration behind Logic 8.

As the director of music-creation product marketing at Apple and the product manager for Logic Studio respectively, Xander Soren and Bill Hunt are well placed to comment on the success of Logic Pro 8 and the suite of software that comes with it. "In terms of the long history of Logic," says Xander, "the release of Logic Studio has been the most successful version of Logic we've ever done!"

Of course, there are many reasons for the success of Logic Studio over the last six months but from a commercial perspective, the dramatic drop in Logic's retail price has arguably caused the biggest impact in the market. What was the thinking behind this?

"What's been important to Apple, and a constant theme throughout our product development, is this idea of the democratisation of technology," enthuses Xander. "We like taking technologies that 10 or 15 years ago would have cost hundreds of thousands of dollars and required lots of specialized hardware and software to work. We take these difficult and expensive technologies, make them easy to use, affordable and available to everybody."

Alongside the price, another distinguishing feature of Logic Studio has been the range of applications and audio content included in the package. "People are blown away by the completeness," says Xander. "You have everything you need, first of all to get started, but also to be able to produce an entire album from start to finish."

For diehard Logic enthusiasts the release of Logic Pro 8 could have easily demonstrated some unwelcome tinkering had Apple not been careful to balance the needs of its existing user base with its vision for the application. "One of the biggest challenges was to move forward and achieve our goals in terms of ease of use," explains Bob, "but not to go too

far away from the core power and flexibility Logic provided." Apple spent a long time looking at the user interface, but also at how users already enjoyed working with the application. "We had time to look at the workflows really carefully," says Xander, "and then made Logic as easy and efficient as possible."

The result is a more elegant and simplified user interface, streamlined to a single operational window. But what has also pleased many long-term Logic users has been the retention of many original features, like the Environment. "There are a lot of Logic users who love the power and flexibility that Logic offers," says Xander. "New users don't need to rely on the Environment, but users that love it still have access to it."

On top of the interface improvements, though, Logic Pro 8 has also introduced new features, as well as improvements to existing tools and plug-ins. "Apple is known for innovation, and we've applied that innovation in a lot of different areas," says Xander. "One of the things we're incredibly pleased with is the Quick Swipe Comping feature," he adds. "It takes time to dig into all these new things," Bob says about the positive reactions he's received. "I'm even now getting emails from people discovering Delay Designer who are completely blown away by it, or Ultrabeat because of the new full view of the sequencer, which makes it easier to set up patterns."

Given the success of its transition into version 8, and the growth in users it's seen in recent months, the future of Logic has never looked brighter, with Apple still hard at work developing their vision of the ultimate DAW.

The release of Logic Studio represents the culmination of several years' hard work aimed at getting Logic out to the wider population.

Logic Platinum 3, 1998
■ By v3, Logic Audio had become a fully fledged native audio/MIDI sequencer with support for a range of audio devices on Mac and PC (including Emagic's own AudioWerk8 card) and real-time plug-in processing. The choice of plug-ins was limited to about 10 items, though.

Logic Platinum 4, 1999
■ Version 4 saw Emagic directing a continuing amount of energy towards plug-ins and virtual instruments. The plug-in folder had swelled with a dizzying array of audio-processing tools alongside a growing collection of optional virtual instruments by Emagic – including the EVP88, ES1, and EXS24. Logic had become a powerful, integrated DAW.

combination of DSP acceleration cards, SCSI hard drives and so on, to turn a Macintosh computer into a complete audio recording and mixing solution. Tapping into the possibilities offered by Digidesign's Pro Tools hardware, Logic users (from version 1.7 onwards) were offered the possibility of using an audio version of Logic – Logic Audio – as the font end to Pro Tools hardware. Indeed, even to this day it's not uncommon to find many professional studios running Digidesign audio hardware with Logic as the front end.

Version 2 of Logic Audio saw the system eventually reach the PC (though it wasn't going to stay there for too long!) with both platforms now encompassing a greater range of audio hardware, including Emagic's own AudioWerk 8 card, rather than just Digidesign's audio hardware. As a result, the concept of the 'native' digital audio workstation, where audio was recorded and mixed entirely using the computer's CPU, started to become a viable proposition.

The rise of the plug-in

Although Emagic can't take the credit for inventing the plug-in – either as an audio processor, or as a virtual instrument – they can certainly say they took full advantage of the concept! Arguably a big part of the success of Logic Audio in the late 90s, and particularly of version 4, was the range of plug-ins that started to be included within the application, including the infamous BitCrusher, Platinum Reverb, and Tape Delay. Software instruments also began to develop, initially with the ES1 synthesizer, and then the EXS24 sampler and various 'vintage' modeled keyboards in the form of the EVP88, EVD6 and EVB3. These instruments, however, weren't included with the application (although they were embedded in the code) but were purchased as 'access codes' stored on Logic's USB-driven XS key.

By the release of Logic Audio 5, both computer recording and Logic itself had come of age. Assuming you had a fast enough computer to run the application, release-quality tracks could be written, recoded and mixed entirely within Logic. In conjunction with Mackie, Emagic had also developed a new hardware control surface specifically designed for Logic – called the Logic Control – with an accompanying automation system clearly influenced by the solutions found on professional flying-fader consoles. Although the Logic Control eventually became a completely cross-platform solution (rebadged as

A strategic alliance with Apogee has enabled Logic Studio to set new standards for native DAW-based recording, offering extremely low latency figures and audiophile conversion technology.

the Mackie Control Universal) it set the standard for DAWs to follow, as well as highlighting just how mature and refined the application had become.

Apple takeover

Arguably the biggest shake up in Logic's history came with Apple's surprise acquisition of Emagic in 2002. Speculation was rife about what this might mean to Logic users, though one outcome – pulling PC support after version 5.5 – became sadly inevitable. On a more positive note, though, the release of the Mac-only Logic Pro 6 in 2004 saw Apple merge the complete suite of optional plug-ins (itself valued at over £1,000) into a single license, making Logic easily the most complete DAW package at any price, as well as providing an attractive crossgrade/upgrade deal for PC users tempted to move over to the Mac platform.

Logic Pro 6 might not have brought any significant developments to Logic itself, but Emagic's programmers – now fully integrated into Apple – had certainly been busy. Under the direction of Gerhard Lengeling, Apple had developed a new application called GarageBand, taking many of the technologies included within Logic, including multitrack recording and editing, virtual instruments, and so on, and packaging them in a simple, easy-to-use music application. A new Loop format, Apple Loops, also allowed pre-recorded loops to be time-stretched and pitch-

> ## "Logic is perfectly placed to take full advantage of the latest developments in computing technology."

shifted quickly and easily, making GarageBand an instant hit with a new generation of computer musicians.

As with all Apple's entry-level media applications, it's clear to see how GarageBand became part of a three-step pathway for audio production. Much like iMovie to Final Cut Pro, GarageBand would entice new users into taking their first steps into audio production – assembling tracks using Apple Loops, as well as using its multi-tracking features to overdub a vocal, for example, or a guitar. For those who were a little more ambitious, a slimmed-down version of Logic, called Logic Express, enabled them to start to explore a professional audio production environment, while the full version, Logic Pro, offered the complete solution to audio production on the Mac.

LOGIC TIMELINE

Logic Platinum 5, 2002

■ For Logic 5, Emagic released a dedicated control surface, the Logic Control, alongside a completely redesigned automation system. But with Apple buying out Emagic, PC support is stopped at v5.5.

Logic Pro 6, 2004

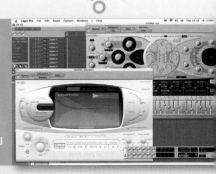

■ Logic Pro 6 was the first release since Apple bought Emagic, yet little had changed with respect to features and functionality. The big news, however, was that Apple had included all the optional plug-ins – Space Designer, the EXS24 and ES2 – as an integral part of the package.

THE EXPANDED UNIVERSE OF LOGIC ON THE MAC
Xander Soren and Bill Hunt talk about GarageBand and MainStage.

One of the most interesting developments with Apple's acquisition of Emagic has been the adaptation of many of Logic's audio technologies into a range of different applications – most notably GarageBand, but also new developments like MainStage.

Developed as part of Apple's iLife package, GarageBand was Apple's attempt at bringing digital music-making to the masses. "GarageBand wasn't specifically designed as a bridge to Logic," explains Xander, "but more about making the best application we could for people just starting in music creation." Arguably a big part of GarageBand's success has been the way it's been designed from ground up, in sharp contrast to the development of other 'Lite' applications. "Other developers take a professional application and turn off features, crippling the application; we thought that was the wrong way to do it," says Xander.

It's easy for professional users to dismiss GarageBand, but it's hard to ignore the wider impact it has had, and the number of people it has introduced to music-making. Indeed, as Xander points out: "GarageBand has become the most widely distributed music software of all time!"

With the increasing importance of music technology on stage, though, it's also interesting to see Apple developing MainStage, a live performance tool based on Logic's instrument and effect technology. Xander explains the motivation behind its inception: "We'd go to some huge concert tours and see people with laptops running Logic, which is deigned to be a DAW, switching through tracks to access their sounds and willing to accept the UI challenges of working with a DAW on stage because they liked the sounds so much!" Bob adds: "It just took one time being at a Madonna concert and watching them open 24 Logic songs and flipping between them to say: maybe we should do something about this!"

The resultant application is one of the standout features in the Logic Studio package, and a product that, on its own, could be well worth the full retail price. "We've already seen some quick adoption," says Xander. "It hasn't even been a year since MainStage came out and we've got people like Kanye West to Madonna all using it."

The Logic universe has grown to become more integral to such a range of musical activities than anybody could have imagined.

Seeing people like Kanye West trying to use Logic live on stage provided the inspiration for Xander and Bill to develop MainStage.

A new, user-friendly Logic
Now fully integrated into the Apple product range, Logic has seen some of its biggest changes in recent years in respect to its user interface and approachability. Certainly, Logic Pro has never been easier to use, with Logic Pro 7 and then Logic Pro 8 being far more in line with the intuitive working process that characterises many of Apple's other products.

The full package has also significantly swelled in size, yet almost inversely dropped in price. Now retitled as Logic Studio, the £319 solution includes the main Logic Pro application, WaveBurner (for CD authoring), MainStage (an innovative solution for using Logic instruments and effects as well as third-party plug-ins live), Soundtrack Pro 2 (the bridging gap between Final Cut Pro and the world of Logic) and an impressive collection of five Jam Packs.

Being so easy to use and affordable means that Logic is still very much alive and well after 15 years of reliable service, with new users joining the fold on a monthly basis. A strategic alliance between Apogee, with their Symphony, Ensemble and Duet audio interfaces, and Apple also makes Logic one of the finest-sounding DAWs out there, and an increasing rival to the dominance of Pro Tools in the professional studio environment.

With Logic as an intrinsic part of the Apple mechanism, the application is now perfectly placed to take full advantage of the latest developments in computing technology, whether it's touch-screen technology migrating from the iPhone (or indeed, an iPhone version of Logic!), or the possible advances offered by the next generation of Macs. It's difficult to predict exactly how Logic itself will change, but it's clear that the application will become even more seamlessly linked to your creative workflow, enabling you to achieve audiophile quality results with increasing ease. MTF

Logic Pro 7, 2004
■ Logic Pro 7 provided the first real indicator of Apple's real intention with the future development of Logic. The user interface got a major facelift and we also saw a number of additional plug-ins added in the form of Sculpture, Ultrabeat and Guitar Amp Pro.

Logic Studio, 2007
■ Logic received arguably the biggest shake-up in its history: Apple slashed the retail price, bundled a number of audio-based applications – including Logic Pro 8 – and audio content under the Logic Studio banner, and completely re-invented the app's user interface to make it far easier for the first-time user.

Apple
LOGIC STUDIO

MusicTech **EXCELLENCE** ★★★★★★★★★★

MusicTech **VALUE**

The latest incarnation of Apple's DAW had been eagerly awaited – and a significant drop in price doubtless broadened its appeal. **Mark Cousins** gets logical.

KEY FEATURES

- Single-window workspace
- Multi-take recording
- Quick Swipe comping
- Comprehensive surround sound support
- XSKey-free operation
- MainStage
- Soundtrack Pro 2
- WaveBurner and compressor
- Impulse response utility
- 5 Jam Packs

LOGIC STUDIO

Manufacturer **Apple**

Price **£319 (Upgrade from Logic Pro or Logic Platinum/Gold 5 or 6: £129)**

Contact **Apple 0800 039 1010**

Web **www.apple.com/uk**

Minimum system requirements
Mac G4 1.25GHz, Mac OSX 10.4.9, 1GB RAM, QuickTime 7.2

There are a number of different DAWs on the market today, but it still seems to be the big three old-timers of computer-based recording – namely, Pro Tools, Logic Pro and Cubase – that stir up the most passionate debate and opinion from their devotees.

Of the three systems, Logic Pro is probably best known for being one of the least approachable DAWs, with its Environments, multiple Editor windows and a relatively uninviting user interface all conspiring to confuse prospective new users. However, for long-term Logic devotees, these same functions are an essential part of the appeal and day-to-day flexibility of the program.

Since it acquired the German developer Emagic in 2002, Apple's development of Logic has been closely watched by its legions of supporters. Logic 6 simply took the software instruments that had previously been sold as optional extras and bundled them with the application.

Logic Pro 7 saw Apple's first attempt at revitalising the user interface, moving from austere blue to utilitarian grey. It also offered a host of additional virtual instruments and plug-ins – Sculpture, Ultrabeat, RingShifter and so on – to help convince us to part with our money.

But what should we expect from the latest incarnation of Logic? Will Apple throw away everything and re-invent the wheel? Will even more virtual instruments inundate us without really addressing core operational issues? Or are we about to witness the next generation of audio production on the Mac?

Studio line

Logic Pro 8 is the principal component of the new package, which now goes under the title of Logic Studio. Of course, WaveBurner was already included with Logic Pro 7, but Apple has significantly swelled the package's size by including Soundtrack Pro 2, MainStage, an impulse response utility, a compressor – for Dolby Digital AC-3 surround encoding and delivery – and all five Jam Packs.

Some components will be more useful than others, but it's certainly an impressive statement of intent, both in terms of functionality and the amount of pre-recorded, high-quality audio content there is on offer to get you started.

Arguably the biggest implication of all these extra goodies is the size of the full install: a massive 46.1GB. Not only does this take up a fair proportion of

MEASURING UP

Apple's decision to slash the price of Logic Pro from £699 to £319 brings the application into direct competition with other platforms. In recent years, Digidesign has invested a lot of effort in bringing Pro Tools LE up to speed with Logic Pro's virtual instruments and plug-ins. The Music Production Toolkit, for example, includes the ES2-like hybrid synthesizer, the Smack! compressor and the TL Space convolution reverb, but this upgrade alone costs £347. Cubase 4 (£649), once the cheaper rival to Logic Pro 7, is now more expensive and lags behind Logic Studio somewhat in terms of virtual instruments and audio content. The price drop could also have an impact on rival PC-based solutions such as Sonar 7 (£369), especially given the Mac's ability to run Windows in Boot Camp mode.

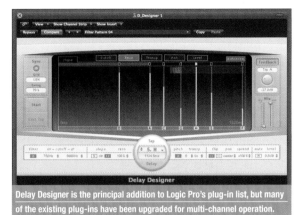

Delay Designer is the principal addition to Logic Pro's plug-in list, but many of the existing plug-ins have been upgraded for multi-channel operation.

your hard drive, but it can also take about an hour or so – patiently watching a progress bar and feeding your Mac an assortment of DVDs as and when prompted – to install. Selecting a custom install and removing the Jam Packs will officially reduce the space required to 5.7GB, though we noted that as little as 3GB was eventually lost from our hard drive's capacity.

Another interesting development is the strategic dropping of Logic's XSKey copy-protection system, particularly given that the rest of the industry is clamouring to adopt iLoks and USB dongles to protecting their software.

SINCE IT ACQUIRED EMAGIC IN 2002, APPLE'S DEVELOPMENT OF LOGIC HAS BEEN CLOSELY WATCHED BY SUPPORTERS.

But there are a few provisos: technically, the licence is for two machines only, and should you have more than one instance of Logic Pro running on a network – and both have the same serial number – you'll receive a stern warning telling you to close one of them down. However, if you've ever lost a dongle, this new-found freedom – and a spare USB port – will be particularly welcome.

The Arrange window

In re-inventing Logic Pro, Apple seems to have directed a large part of its attention towards making the program more approachable for the first-time user. The biggest change is to the Arrange window, which has effectively merged all of Logic's previous windows – mixers, matrix editors, audio window, sample editors and so on – into a single interface. Individual versions of these windows remain, but the implied concept is that you spend most of your time working from the combined interface rather than constantly switching between windows. If you need the mixer, for example, simply click on the Mixer tab and the mixer will slide into place below your arrangement. When you're finished, close the tab and the mixer slides out of the way.

Despite being fans of Logic Pro's old configurable user interface, we have to admit to being won over by the tangible functional improvements this combined Arrange window offers. For example, the

library, which pops up on the right side of the screen along with the Media Bin and List editors, enables you to browse plug-in settings in list form, rather than having to keep delving into the plug-in's interface. Equally, the Inspector, which contains the sequencer and instrument parameters of old, now includes an additional fader as well as the main channel fader to illustrate the signal flow to a subsequent buss or main output fader. Following this concept a stage further, the audio mixer can now be set to Single mode, illustrating the signal path for the selected channel.

Two permanent additions to the Arrange page include the toolbar and transport bar, which sit at the top and bottom of the page respectively. Although we liked being able to customise the settings – which, in the case of the toolbar, adds quick access to functions previously accessible only via long-winded menus or key commands – they do make for a more crowded working environment on smaller screens. We also missed the ability to access a floating Extended Sequence Parameters window, which now seems to be permanently embedded in the Inspector.

Audio editing

While Logic has always been a competent platform when it came to MIDI and virtual instruments, the same cannot be said of its audio-editing capabilities and its ability to deal with multiple takes. Both these shortcomings have been significantly overhauled in Logic Pro 8, with a new system – Take folders – in place for multiple takes, and Quick Swipe comping facilitated as a means of assembling recordings into a finished piece.

Take folders can be created in two ways: either automatically, whenever you record in Cycle mode; or manually, by packing several regions into a Take folder. In certain respects, Take folders bear some resemblance to Pro Tools'

METHOD SPOT

Comparing the DSP efficiency of Logic Pro 7 to that of Logic Pro 8 will be an important consideration for users working on G5 Macs. On a single-processor 1.9GHz G5, we were able to run up to seven instances of the DSP-hungry Sculpture in Logic Pro 7 without getting a Core Audio overload error. The same session in Logic Pro 8 produced similar performance results, with only the eighth instance of Sculpture pushing the system into overload – as it did in version 7. The DSP meter, however, appears to deliver a more peaky reading in Logic Pro 8, despite running the same number of instances.

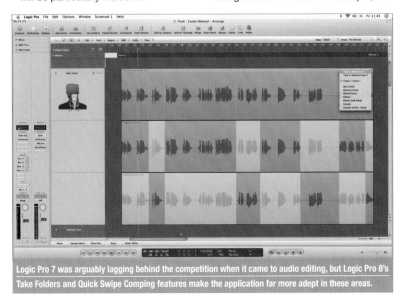

Logic Pro 7 was arguably lagging behind the competition when it came to audio editing, but Logic Pro 8's Take Folders and Quick Swipe Comping features make the application far more adept in these areas.

Playlist system, which enables you to move between alternate takes without having to run parallel track lanes. However, Logic's powerful new editing abilities become apparent when you start comping your various takes together.

By temporarily 'exploding' the Take folder you can see each pass. These can be used to create a comp simply by dragging the appropriate area of each take as required. When you're finished, simply close the Take folder and carry on as before, or flatten the edits to render the comped track as a set of regions.

Along with these major editing improvements, there's also plenty to get excited about as far as the more minor refinements are concerned: Tab to Transients, sample-level editing in the Arrange window and more contextual menus. Ultimately, it all makes audio editing in Logic Pro 8 a strength of the application rather than a weakness – even to the point of rivalling the finesse of Pro Tools in this area.

Delay Designer

Surprisingly, given the deluge of instruments and effects we've seen in the last two Logic updates, Logic Studio offers little in the way of additional plug-ins. You do, however, get a new Delay Designer, which enables you to build

Once you've finished a surround mix, you can bounce directly to DVD-A or use the Compressor application to render an AC-3 Dolby Digital version of your mix.

Added extras

Although we've concentrated mostly on Logic Studio's key applications, it would be remiss not to highlight at least some of the other new elements. MainStage, for example, finally offers a solution to the shortcomings of using Logic live on stage, either as a guitarist – using Guitar Amp Pro and its various effects – or as a keyboard player wanting to access Logic's virtual instruments.

The concept behind MainStage is that you design your own patches, layering together various instruments and effects with associated macro controls – all MIDI-controllable – for primary functions like filter cutoff and resonance. While you're performing, a high-contrast interface enables you to move between patches while visualising key parameters, dynamic keyboard splits and so on.

If you're short of inspiration, there's no doubt that the amount of free sound content significantly adds to the value of the package. Usefully, the five Jam Packs – which still retail at £69 each – cover a wide range of genres and

Logic's Ultrabeat has received some much-needed attention; it now features a completely revised soundbank and new Step Automation mode.

Logic users into the fold, all of whom will be increasingly keen to upgrade to a shiny new Intel Core Duo machine…

For existing Logic users, though, there's still plenty to like about Logic Studio. Despite fears of features such as Environments disappearing altogether, Apple has retained these important elements of professional functionality.

Sure, you will need time to adjust, but the improvements to workflow and its audio capabilities take Logic into the next generation of audio sequencing. Of course, opinion will still be divided as to which is the best DAW, but no other DAW currently offers this level of functionality for the money. **MTF**

ARGUABLY APPLE'S BIGGEST STRATEGIC SHIFT HAS BEEN ITS DECISION TO SLASH LOGIC'S PRICE FROM £699 TO £319.

your own custom arrangement of tapped delays, each with their own pan, cutoff, resonance and transposition settings. It's also good to see some attention lavished on Ultrabeat, which now has a decent soundbank and an intriguing new Step Automation mode. Several new algorithms are also available to the compressor, including VCA, FET and opto operation.

The biggest change in respect to plug-ins has been in the implementation of true surround sound integration. Although surround mixing was possible in Logic Pro 7, the lack of a decent surround panner – and, more importantly, true multi-channel plug-ins – left Logic Pro's 5.1 mixing trailing behind applications like Pro Tools. Now, however, you get an enhanced surround panner, surround metering and downmixing, plus surround versions of Space Designer, the Compressor, Delay Designer and all the modulation effects.

instrumentation rather than just offering generic dance loops. And if you're working in post production, Soundtrack Pro 2 could also come in handy as a bridge between your Logic work and audio dubs created in Final Cut Pro.

Mass appeal

Although it's easy to get absorbed in the wealth of functional improvements and additions in Logic Studio, arguably Apple's biggest strategic shift – and a move that could send tremors through the rest of the industry – is its decision to slash Logic's price.

At £699, Logic Pro 7 was clearly pitched at professional users who could easily justify spending the best part of £1,000 on an application they would be using on a daily basis. At £319, though, Logic Studio is an entirely different proposition: an accessible, flexible and inspiring tool for anyone making music on a Mac. Of course, Apple is well aware that this can only bring more

SUMMARY

WHY BUY
- Less than half the price of Logic Pro 7
- Significantly easier to use interface
- Improved audio editing, plus efficient take management
- Impressive quantity of bundled audio content
- MainStage offers a fantastic solution for playing live with instruments and effects
- Improved OMF compatibility, AC-3 export and 5.1 support
- No dongle protection

WALK ON BY
- Full install takes over 46GB
- Transport and toolbar permanently fixed to the Arrange window
- No floating Extended Sequence Parameters window
- That new 8-core Mac Pro looks increasingly hard to resist…

VERDICT

Boasting a significantly improved interface, restructured pricing and plenty of audio content, this is Apple's big push to bring Logic to the masses. If you've got a Mac and enjoy making music, then Logic Studio has to be considered an essential purchase.

★★★★★★★★★★

METHOD SPOT

MainStage provides the ideal middle ground between your dedicated MIDI or USB controller and Logic's array of instruments and effects. First, you'll need to create a custom layout based on your controller – in essence, a virtual representation of your controller, complete with keyboard, pots, footswitches and so on. Next, map the pots and faders on your controller to the virtual controllers on screen. The virtual controllers can then be mapped to the associated controls in the plug-in's interface. Now, irrespective of which plug-in you switch to, your MIDI controller will produce the same sonic result.

Logic Studio. See how it sounds.

Free Logic Studio workshops this Autumn

Aug 28th @ 6.00	London ,SAE Institute	Computer Warehouse	020 8400 1298
Sept 3rd @ 3.00	London, Design Council	Square Group	020 7692 6810
Sept 9th @ 6.30	Guilford Academy, of Contempary Music	Andertons Music	01483 456733
*Sept 16th @ 6.30	West London, Digital Village	Digital Village	020 8992 5592
*Sept 17th @ 2.00 and 4.00	Birmingham, Digital Village	Digital Village	0121 687 4777
*Sept 18th @ 6.30	Bristol, Digital Village	Digital Village	0117 946 7700
*Sept 20th @ 1.00 and 3.00	East London, Digital Village	Digital Village	01708 771991
Sept 25th @ 6.30	Plymouth, University of Plymouth	Stormfront	0800 612 1044
Sept 25th @ 6.30	Nottingham, Trent FM Arena	KRCS	0115 941 5675
Oct 9th @ 6.30	Reading, Dawsons Music	Dawsons Music	0118 958 1320
Oct. 16th @ 6:30	Liverpool, SAE Institute	Dawsons Music	0151 709 1455

* Digital Village events feature special guest artist Steve Jones (Air, Brian Eno, Herbie Hancock)

For further schedule information and to register, please see the Events Listing at:

www.apple.com/uk/hotnews

Using Logic Pro

Getting to grips with Logic Pro isn't as complicated as it might first appear – and the creative rewards make it well worth the effort! **Mark Cousins** gets you started.

With the release of Logic 8, Apple has achieved the seemingly impossible feat of making a DAW as vast as Logic fit with the intuitive, easy-to-use workflow that characterises many of its other applications. However, if you are new to computer music production in general – maybe having migrated from GarageBand – or if you are more used to working with another audio application,

there's still a lot to get to grips with, and the task of putting together your first track can be an occasionally fraught experience. In this feature, therefore, we're going to explore Logic from a first-time user's perspective, showing you the quickest and easiest ways to take a project from the seeds of an idea to a complete mix.

A new project

All tracks in Logic begin from the New Project window (File>New Project). The term 'project' actually brings

IN THIS FEATURE, WE'RE GOING TO EXPLORE LOGIC FROM A FIRST-TIME USER'S PERSPECTIVE.

together all the various media files – along with the song file – that are associated with a track. When you create a project, therefore, Logic is effectively creating a folder, inside of which there will be an Audio Files folder, your song data, samples files and so on, all neatly organised for archiving later on. The New Project dialogue box contains a number of pre-assigned templates that provide some starting points for certain styles of music or production

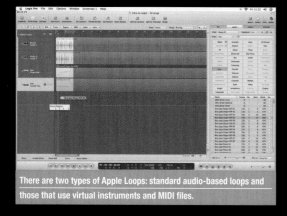

There are two types of Apple Loops: standard audio-based loops and those that use virtual instruments and MIDI files.

activity, though in most cases the Empty Project option is probably your most suitable starting point.

Once you've created an empty project – and assuming Logic has prompted you already – remember to create your first save using the Save As… option in the File menu. Given that you're working with a blank canvas, Logic will also ask you to create your first track. This could be an Audio track, if you intend to record from an input on your audio interface; a Software Instrument track, if you intend to use Logic's own virtual instruments, such as the EXS24 Sampler; or an External MIDI track, if you intend to use Logic to control hardware synthesizers or samplers. Of course, you can add any type of track into a project at any point simply by using the small plus sign on the top of the track list.

The Arrange window

Logic's Arrange window is where the majority of your production activities will take place. Operationally, the main things to notice about the Arrange window are the various functional areas and editors that spring up to the left, right and bottom of the main window. For example, we have the Inspector to the left of the Arrange area, which enables us to inspect aspects of our song such as individual channels of our mixer and information relating to each track or region in the project. To the bottom, alongside the transport controls, there are tabs for each of the principle editors, such as the Piano Roll Editor, the

Logic's main interface has four areas: a central Arrange area, an Inspector to the left, Editors at the bottom, and Media Files to the right.

Score Editor and, of course, the Mixer section, which brings the different elements of your track together.

To the right of the Arrange area you can find what is called the Audio Bin (Window>Audio Bin). This is principally used to display a long list of the audio files associated with your project. It is also a good place to ▶

LOGIC'S ARRANGE WINDOW IS WHERE THE MAJORITY OF YOUR PRODUCTION ACTIVITIES WILL TAKE PLACE.

STEP-BY-STEP Recording and editing audio in Logic.

1 To record audio into Logic, you must first create an accompanying audio track using the small plus sign on the top of the track list. Select Audio from the list of possible track types and choose the input that corresponds to the input your instrument is plugged into.

2 Once you've created your track, you can name it by double-clicking on the track's name in the track list. Record-enabling the track – which is done by using the small R – will enable you to set the level of your input using the mixer's meters as a guide.

3 To begin recording, simply locate the area of the song you want to work on and press Record on the Transport bar. You will get a one-bar count-in before recording begins. You might also want to activate the click using the Metronome icon on the Transport bar.

4 If you want to do another take, simply drag back the Song Position pointer and record directly over your first take. Though this looks destructive, you will still be able to go back to the original recording, or even use different parts of each take.

5 By overdubbing, you will have created a Take folder. To unpack this and see its contents, click on the small arrow in the top left corner of the region. By 'swiping' across the various regions you can build up a comp of components from each take.

6 If you're happy with your comp, you can close it down using the same arrow that you used to open the folder. Alternatively, you can use the arrow on the right to permanently 'flatten' the comp so you can adjust the crossfades and so on.

demonstrate one way of starting a track and the application of Apple Loops, though, of course, you can start a project in any way you see fit – using a drum break from Ultrabeat, for example, or simply recording a song from scratch.

Once the Audio Bin is open, you can access the Apple Loops in your system by pressing the Loops tab. Use the accompanying Loop Browser to find what best suits your creative juices, and then drag your chosen loop over to a blank part of the Arrange area to have Logic automatically create a corresponding track. The Apple Loop's icon also indicates the two varieties of loops – the blue wave indicates audio files, while the green note indicates a MIDI-based Apple Loop. Either of the Apple Loop formats will conform to your project's existing tempo.

Structuring your track

When you've assembled a number of Apple Loops into your Arrange window, you can start to experiment with how they're pieced together. As is true of any DAW, Logic presents the components of a song as a series of regions that can be freely moved around the Arrange area to create the finished structure of the track. Holding down [Alt] on your keyboard as you move one or more regions enables you to make a copy. There are also various additional tools – scissors, mute and so on – that can extend what you can achieve here. You can call these tools up at any point by pressing the [Escape] key.

As well as manipulating the regions in the Arrange area, you can also use the Inspector (the keyboard shortcut is [I]) to access some simple editing features on a region-by-region basis. For example, rather than endlessly copying a region, try selecting the region, opening the Inspector, and adjusting the region's parameters to set it to loop. Note that you can suspend the loop at any point in the arrangement later on by clicking in the top half of the greyed-out region.

Depending on the type of region you've got selected, you'll also find number of further options in the Inspector. On the whole, audio regions are rather limited, but with MIDI-based regions you'll find options like quantizing, velocity, dynamics and so on, that will change how the region is played back.

Fix it in the mix

Once you've built up the structure of your song, you'll undoubtedly want to turn your attention to mixing it: balancing each of the tracks and possibly adding further effects like EQ, compression or reverb. The Mixer tab at

ONCE YOU'VE BUILT THE STRUCTURE OF YOUR SONG YOU CAN TURN YOUR ATTENTION TO MIXING IT.

STEP-BY-STEP Playing, recording and editing virtual instruments.

1 To work with a virtual instrument in Logic, you'll need to create a new Software Instrument track. You can then instantiate an appropriate instrument under the I/O tab of the instrument's mixer channel – the EVP88 electric piano, for example, or the EXS24 sampler.

2 With the instrument loaded, you'll probably want to explore the presets to find a sound that suits your objectives. Open the Bin and click on the Library tab to see the list of presets for the currently selected instrument.

3 To record a keyboard part for your instrument, select the track and press Record. Unlike audio recordings, MIDI recordings don't fall into the Quick Swipe take folder system, so you might want to use multiple tracks [Alt+Apple+S] to manage the various takes.

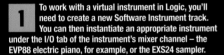

4 To quantize your performance quickly, open the Inspector, select the MIDI region(s) in question, and select one of the dropdown quantize options from the Quantize menu. The various letters in the swing quantize settings denote the amount of shuffle applied.

5 If you need to edit the MIDI data further, open the Piano Roll editor using the tab at the bottom of the Arrange window. Now any selected region will be displayed in the editor, with notes being repositioned or copied using the standard techniques.

6 Beyond the basic position and pitch of notes, you might also want to explore editing aspects such as velocity. Use the Piano Roll editor's own set of tools (accessible via the [Escape] key) to select the Velocity tool. Click on a note and drag it up or down.

THERE'S A WHOLE NEW WORLD OF POSSIBILITIES AVAILABLE TO YOU ONCE YOU START RECORDING YOUR OWN MATERIAL.

the bottom of the Arrange window opens up Logic's virtual mixer. This has a channel for each of the corresponding tracks in your arrangement, an output fader and a master fader. First you'll want to concentrate on the level and pan settings for each track, ideally building a coherent mix that doesn't distort the main outputs. If the combined levels are too hot, consider reducing the master control to restore some headroom.

Adding plug-ins to the empty Insert slots will enable you to modify the sound of each track and to double-click the EQ box to quickly establish some suitable equalization settings. As you'll see from the list of plug-ins, all of which are organised into various categories, Logic comes with enough audio processing technology to create a complete professional mix. Double-clicking on any plug-in will enable you to change its relative settings, or browse through its presets, to find an output that gets the results you want.

Use your own combination of plug-ins, instantiated across a mixer channel, to change the sound and timbre of each track.

We've only just begun…

Of course, what we have looked at here is only just the beginning of what can be achieved with Logic. Although we have covered the overarching principles of the Arrange window and mixing, there's a whole new world of possibilities available to you once you start recording some of your own material – either as audio tracks from acoustic or electric instruments, or by controlling Logic's own virtual instruments using MIDI information. Whichever method you choose, you'll soon appreciate that working with Logic – as with music itself – is an endless journey of discovery, with new creative possibilities opening up on a daily basis! **MTF**

STEP-BY-STEP Completing your first track by creating a mix.

1 You can open the mixer at any point using the tab at the bottom of the Arrange window, or [X] on the keyboard. The mixer is essentially a vertical representation of your arrangement, laid out according to the order of the tracks in your track list.

2 Use EQ and Compression as your main mix tools. EQ can be activated from the top of the channel strip and enables you to shape the timbre of a sound. Use the Compressor plug-in to control the dynamic range of important instruments like bass or vocals.

3 Reverb is best applied using a send from a channel so a number of instruments can share different amounts of the same reverb. Under the Sends section, create a series of new sends to Bus 1. The level for each channel's reverb can be controlled via the small pot.

4 In creating the bus sends, Logic will have also created an accompanying aux master fader, which can be used as the location for the reverb. Instantiate Space Designer on this aux master, and you should now hear the reverb on the tracks being sent through.

5 Another use of aux faders is to compress groups of sounds. In this case, send the required tracks directly out to a spare bus under the I/O tabs. With the track routed, you can then instantiate a compressor across the corresponding aux fader.

6 With the mix complete, you'll need to render it as a finished file. To do this, click on the Bounce (Bnce) tab on the main output fader. A dialogue box will enable you to specify the length of the bounce and the file format – a 24-bit WAV is probably the best choice.

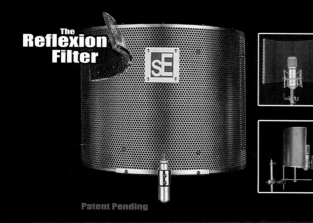
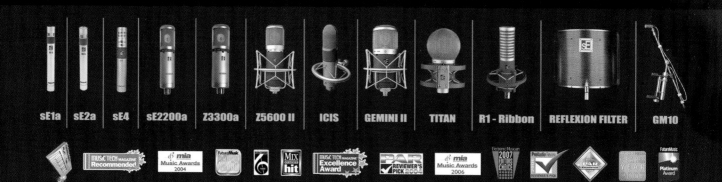

Vocal processing & production

With Logic's army of special effects, and dedicated processors for trouble-shooting, any vocal recording can be made to shine. **Mo Volans** gets vocal.

Vocal production is a vast subject area. There are engineers who dedicate their entire careers to the subject and there are producers who regularly hire specialists just to achieve the perfect vocal mix. There's a lot to learn about vocal processing – we can't cover more than the basics here – and producing a vocal yourself might seem a daunting prospect, but if you are armed with the right knowledge and a firm understanding of the correct uses of the plethora of Logic plug-ins geared for vocal processing, the job can be tackled with ease.

You may be using vocal samples from vinyl and CD, or you could be recording performances yourself; either way it is quite likely that a basic level of processing will be needed to bring things up to speed. Many of Logic's generic plug-ins are perfectly suited to supplying generic treatments such as compression, gating, equalization and saturation, but there are also processors that are designed especially for treating vocals. Some of these dedicated processors are used for restoration or repair, while others produce more creative effects that can be employed in totally transforming your vocal sound.

WITH THE RIGHT KNOWLEDGE AND LOGIC PLUG-INS THE JOB CAN BE TACKLED WITH EASE.

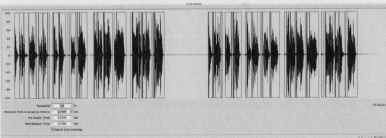

Power Tip

Once you're happy with the way your vocal is sounding you can add some polish. Adding reverb not only gives vocals more space and sheen but will often help them site in the mix. Even small amounts of room or plate reverb can make a huge difference to a well-treated vocal and it's not uncommon to see specific vocal reverb presets. Logic's Space Designer is no exception with some really excellent vocal reverbs on offer.

When it comes to deciding what forms of processing to apply to your vocal, your attention should be firmly focused on any problem areas of the recording. Once any issues are fixed and the file is restored to its full potential, further processing can be applied without fear of any adverse results.

The following are some examples of possible issues you may come across when tackling an untreated vocal, along with suggestions for how to address them:

Sibilance

Over-emphasised 's', 'sh' and 'ch' sounds in vocal recordings are called 'sibilants'. They are caused by the performer constricting their vocal tract with their lips and so restricting the outflow of air. What this means to you is the occurrence of high frequency peaks, generally between 5kHz and 10 kHz. These need to be controlled.

Logic includes a dedicated processor for dealing with sibilance called the De-esser. This is extremely effective in reducing problem areas for both male and female ▶

voices. If you're not sure how to operate the De-esser, try Logic's presets as a starting point.

Pops

If a decent pop shield wasn't used during recording, you may experience thumps of low-frequency sound cutting through your vocal mix. Obviously, the most sensible option here would be to re-record the part using the appropriate kit, but if you don't have that luxury, or you are working with vocal samples, there are still things that can be done.

ONE THING YOU CAN'T AVOID IS SINGERS BREATHING AND GENERALLY MAKING NOISE DURING THEIR PERFORMANCE.

Though there are no dedicated tools for tackling the problem of 'pops and thumps', you may want to try manually editing the transients they cause in an audio editor. If this doesn't help, experiment with a mixture of high-pass filtering and multi-compression.

Rumble

In a perfect world, all vocals would be recorded in an isolated booth using a de-coupling shock mount. In the real world, however, things don't always work that way

and sounds from the outside world are introduced into our performances.

One of most common unwanted artefacts that occurs due to poor recording technique is low-frequency rumble. This problem is easily tackled using Logic's high-pass filter to remove frequencies below about 150Hz. Caution should be used here to ensure that none of the vocal's lower frequencies are removed in the process.

Distortion and clipping

Unfortunately, this is pretty much an irreversible process that can easily crop up while you're recording and processing a vocal file. Short of re-recording the take – if that's an option – there is not a huge amount you can do, though the filtering of problem frequencies and the manual editing of clipped areas will go some way towards alleviating the situation.

Breathing and noise

One thing you can't avoid is singers breathing and generally making noise during their performance. Most of the time, any background noise is masked by signal but in gaps between words and phrases you may want to remove unwanted sound. If this is the case, a noise gate is your best option.

Logic supplies two noise gates at two levels of complexity, so you should find one of them suitable for

---

STEP-BY-STEP Applying basic vocal processing.

1 Import the vocal you wish to process into its own track and inspect it for problem areas to determine what treatments are needed. Create a duplicate track and copy the vocal file onto it. This will leave you with a dry version of your vocal for reference.

2 The first thing to tackle is any background noise and breathing. This is achieved by using a noise gate. Once you have found a threshold setting that eliminates all the unwanted signal, set the attack and release times so that all the vocal performance is heard.

3 Next use a high-pass filter or EQ to remove any rumble and low-frequency interference that may have been picked up during recording. This should clean up the vocal considerably and enable you to focus on the more important frequencies.

4 Now use a compressor to control the overall dynamics of the performance. This is possibly the most important part of any vocal signal path, as it ensures that all parts of the recording are audible and that there are no overwhelming peaks.

5 If needed, use an EQ to add some 'air' to the signal by adding some upper-mids and high end. Also remove any overbearing frequencies that may inhibit the vocal's presence in your mix. The culprits tend to be low-mids and nasal sounds around 1kHz and above.

6 The extra dynamics processing and equalization you have added can enhance any sibilance that may be present. Using a de-esser will help to suppress any spikes here and ensure that the overall vocal sound is well rounded and easy on the ear.

your needs. Even the less complex Silver Gate has enough parameters to solve the worst noise issues.

Squash and tweak

An integral part of any vocal effects chain is dynamic control. We achieve this with the all-important Compressor. Logic's Compressor is a true all-rounder and, with features such as output distortion, vintage modelling and wet/dry mixing, it packs more than enough punch to level even the wildest vocal tracks.

Don't be afraid to use pretty large amounts of gain reduction here and, again, try using presets as a sensible starting point, tweaking them as you go. Once you're happy with the overall dynamic response of the vocal track you can finish the treatment off by using the Compressor's in-built limiter circuit or Logic's stand-alone Limiter plug-in.

At this point the vocal may need some light EQ to add some air or reduce any unpleasant nasal qualities. Logic's standard channel EQ is fine here and will introduce only small amounts of latency. The linear phase version requires much more CPU power to operate.

Special FX

Some of the most interesting vocal effects in Logic are those intended to manipulate your audio in a creative fashion. For instance, Logic includes vocoder and vocal

Power Tip

A useful alternative to noise gates for removing large areas of noise and silence is Logic's Detect Silence feature. By selecting the vocal part and navigating to the Audio menu in the Arrange window, you can access the Detect Silence editing screen. This resembles Logic's Audio Editor and can determine threshold, attack and release settings. Set correctly, silence between phrases – and any noise – will be removed, leaving you with just the parts you want.

transformer plug-ins that can be used to twist things beyond recognition if desired. These take a bit of getting used to but, once mastered, some great alternative versions of your vocals can be created.

There are a few other dedicated vocal plug-ins that blur the line between corrective and creative effects, such as Logic's Pitch Correction processor. This can obviously be used for its intended purpose – to knock less than perfect notes into shape – but it can also generate synthesised 'Cher'-like effects when pushed.

There's more, but you can already see that Logic 8 supplies a great collection of plug-ins for processing and manipulating your vocals in a large number of ways. MTF

STEP-BY-STEP Using special FX to twist a vocal part.

1 Again, use a noise gate to eliminate any unwanted background and breath noises. This will enable any processors to clamp down on the parts of the signal that are important. If unchecked, this noise will be enhanced by plug-ins added later in the chain.

2 Logic's Vocal Enhancer plug-in is great for adding extra harmonics and processed edge to your vocal. This plug-in not only has an enhancement circuit but also includes speaker correction, for use with voices recorded on small speakers and systems.

3 Try Logic's Pitch Correction for creating pitch-based effects by turning the response time down to minimum and removing some notes from the default selection to manipulate the pitch. This will totally change the tuning of your performance so take your time.

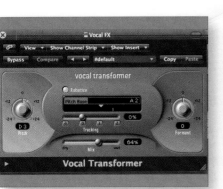

4 Possibly the most drastic vocal processor is Logic's Vocal Transformer, which enables vocoder-style drones to be created with its Robotic mode. The vocal's formant can also be changed, enabling the vocal to be made higher or deeper in tone without changing its pitch.

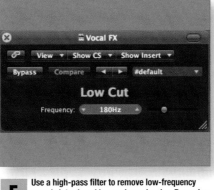

5 Use a high-pass filter to remove low-frequency sounds introduced by previous plug-ins. Removing everything below around 100-200Hz is about right but be sure you don't remove too much or you will end up with a weak, thin-sounding end result.

6 Finally, compress the whole thing to get everything in check dynamically. Settings will vary vastly when compressing FX and presets may not be as much use here as they are with a more traditional vocal, so you may have to program things from scratch.

LOGIC PRO 8 WORKSHOP

ON YOUR *MusicTech* DVD ROM
Full-sized screenshots and all the supporting files you'll need to follow this tutorial.

ARRANGE WINDOW SECRETS

Before delving too deeply into the complexities of Logic, it's worth spending time learning the wonders of the Arrange window. **Mark Cousins** makes arrangements.

The Arrange window is very much the centrepiece of your creative workflow in Logic 8, especially now that so many of the previous additional windows – the Matrix Editor, the Audio Mixer and so on – have all been unified under the one interface. However, though this simplification of Logic's layout means that the principle functions included within the Arrange window are now much easier to find, there are still plenty of features that are easy to miss, additional functionality that is easy to overlook, and some hidden tricks within the application that, unless you know where to look, are sometimes only discovered by accident rather than design. In this workshop, therefore, we're going to round up some of these lesser-known features and lift the lid on some new and exciting ways of working with Logic.

The folder system

Let's start by looking at some of the features and functions that are easy to overlook. The most important of these has to be the folder system, which not only enables you to look at the Arrange window in a new way, but which also offers a revised approach to mixing in Logic, especially where you need to deal with lots of tracks.

Logic's folder system enables you to pack and unpack any number of audio and/or MIDI regions in the Arrange window down to a single folder on its own track. To create a folder, select the regions you wish to include and press [Apple+F] or go to Region>Folder>Pack Folder.

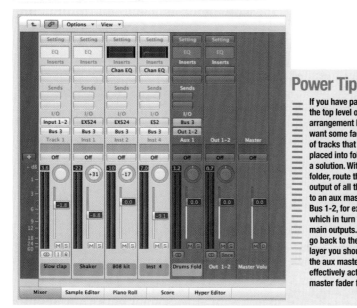

Of course, you can rename the folder or the folder track accordingly, and though all the parts have been neatly packed away, they will still play back as if they were on the top level of the Arrange window. To view the contents of the folder, simply double-click on the region and then use the small 'back' arrow to step back to the root level of the arrangement. **1**

Creating folders is easy, and that's good news in itself, but what's really interesting is how the folder system can have various positive effects on your workflow and productivity. One of my favourite uses of the folder system is as a temporary 'bin' for a project. Tracks or regions that have no apparent use can be dragged to a pre-packed folder called Bin. This keeps them out of sight and out of the way, but they are still recallable later on if you find that you do have a use for them after all. To access these files you could unpack the entire contents of your Bin folder or, better still, you could cut/copy specific tracks or regions from your Bin folder and paste them into the main arrangement.

Perhaps the best use of folders, though, is as a means of organising your mixer. As the Mixer area handles the folder system in almost exactly the same way as the Arrange window – even down to displaying a folder track – you can effectively divide your mix up into a series of layers, or groups of instruments, using the folder functionality to navigate the mix. **2**

And if leftover tracks from a packed folder bother you, you can always use the function Track>Delete Unused to clear any newly emptied tracks from the Arrange window.

Extended region parameters

Another set of useful productivity tools you will not want to overlook is the Arrange window's 'extended region parameters'. These significantly add to what you can achieve with MIDI regions using the Inspector. To view the extended region parameters select View>Extended Region Parameters and look across to the Inspector to see the updated and extended set of options. **3**

The extended parameters are mainly orientated towards quantizing, building on and refining the fairly crude set of controls you're provided with when you first open the Inspector. One of the most useful of these is the Q-Strength parameter, which softens the quantize down from its initial setting in the top of the region parameters box. A 50% strength, for example, will only move notes halfway to their quantize position, thereby keeping part of the feel of the original performance.

The Q-Flam parameter is a good option if you're working with guitar samples, where on-the-beat

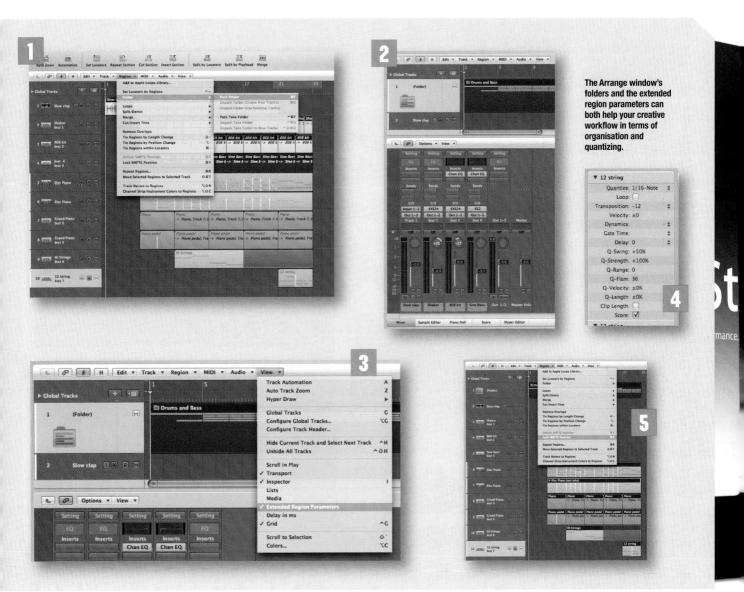

The Arrange window's folders and the extended region parameters can both help your creative workflow in terms of organisation and quantizing.

quantizing can sound unnatural. By setting a 'flamed' offset, the grouped notes will be spread out, with increasingly higher figures spacing the notes apart to a greater degree. **4**

Lock/Unlock SMPTE Position

The Lock/Unlock SMPTE Position, which you'll find under the Region menu, is another important feature that can easily be overlooked. Although initially conceived as a way of locking sound effects to pictures, I've also found several useful music applications that I use on a daily basis. One of the best of these is the ability to time-freeze audio and MIDI regions before you carry out tempo modifications – particularly half-time or double-time tempo changes, such as 70bpm to 140bpm and vice versa. With the regions frozen, any changes in tempo won't affect the length or speed of data contained within. All audio regions, for example, could get doubled or halved in size, and once you've set the new tempo, the regions can be unlocked to restore the original tempo-based functionality of Logic. **5**

Another variation is to use an empty region as an alterative source of marker, either to mark a given point in time – such as a commercial cut ending at 29.5 seconds,

for example – or a given duration. Again, the SMPTE Lock keeps the region's exact position and relative length, irrespective of the song's tempo. This enables you to find the exact number of bars, for example, that will play before you hit a given time point. **6**

Demixing

The demixing feature (Region>Demix by Event Pitch, or Region>Demix by Event Channel) works more or less in the opposite way to the folder feature: it explodes a MIDI region into its constituent note-based parts. The Event Pitch option, for example, takes the region and splits it ▶

Power Tip

If you've been creating complicated glitch and stutter effects that you want to use in your track, you may well have found it difficult to manage these in relation to a larger arrangement – regions can sometimes get lost or dropped in the duplication process. Consider packing the regions up, either as part of a take folder (Region>Folder>Pack Take Folder) or as a traditional folder (Region>Folder> Pack Folder).

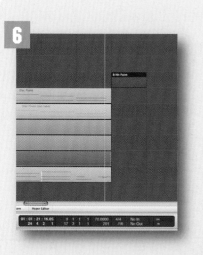

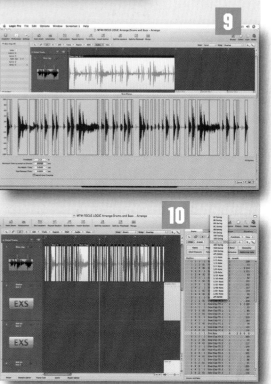

Using Logic's existing tools in new ways can open up new possibilities. Try exploring demixing as a means of splitting chords into single monophonic lines; and try using the Strip Silence tool and quantizing in the Event List editor to experiment with grooves in your audio files.

▶ into several new regions based on each note pitch in the sequence. This functionality is obviously orientated towards drum sequences, where each note represents a different part of the kit. Once demixed in this way, you could choose to repack the regions as a folder, keeping the split notes but tidying the sequence away. **7**

An even more exciting use of demixing, though, is the Event Channel option, especially when this is used with the Voices to Channels feature and chordal sequences in the Piano Roll editor. In this example, you need to open the region in the Piano Roll Editor and apply the option Functions>Note Events>Voices to Channels. Closing down the editor, you can then use the Event Channel Demixing option, which will result in your original chord being split into a series of monophonic lines. Try sending each of these lines to a different software instrument to build a harmonic procession through a series of interwoven layers, rather than just block chords. **8**

Audio quantizing

It's interesting to note just how many of Logic's more intriguing and powerful features can be discovered by twisting and adapting its existing tools in a creative way. One really good example of this is audio quantizing direct from the Arrange window, which is an alternative to using the solution suggested in Logic's Sample Editor (Factory> Quantize Engine).

First, you'll need to split the audio region into its constituent hits by using the Audio>Strip Silence function. Now adjust the threshold setting to achieve the best and most accurate set of stripped regions, ideally having a different region for each hit in the drum loop. As an alternative, you can always use the [Alt] keyboard modifier as you make a 16th slice, which will place 16th edits throughout the entire duration of the region. **9**

Once you've sliced the original region, select all the individual hits and open the Event list (View>List). From here, you should be able to pull down the Quantize menu and select an appropriate setting – applying a slight shuffle to a rigid 1/16th groove, for example, or tightening up a played loop to a more rigid time division. (It's a shame, though, that you can't use the Q-Strength control here.) In some extreme cases, you might need to perform some corrective surgery to rectify a few clicks or glitches, either applying crossfades to smooth transitions, or using the Region Tie feature (Region>Tie Regions by Length Change) to remove any small gaps. **10**

Logic Pro is a well-developed application and there's always a variety of ways to solve any creative dilemma, as well a raft of features and possibilities that few of us have anywhere near enough time to fully explore. Thinking creatively about how you use the application, therefore, as well as experimenting with features and tools you might have dismissed as not useful, can bring many new possibilities to the way you work with Logic, and ultimately, to the quality of the music you produce. **MTF**

Power Tip

One of the interesting things to note about the folder system is how it behaves with looped regions embedded within the folder. Technically speaking, a folder will only ever be as big as the last 'physical' region in the sequence, so if all the regions are set to loop, the folder might only be two or four bars in length. In this case, the duration of the loop is now defined by the folder length. You can extend the folder to make the loops last longer.

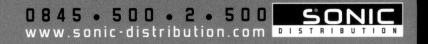

ON YOUR
MusicTech DVD
ROM
Full-sized screenshots and all the supporting files you'll need to follow this tutorial.

LOGIC PRO 7 WORKSHOP

SUBBASS AND EXCITER

Do you ever find that your mixes lack some of the subsonic depth or crystal-clear highs of a commercial recording? **Mark Cousins** investigates a special solution.

Although the standard of most project studio mixes is good, they can lack the sheen and power of a commercial mix, mainly in respect to the two extremes of the audio spectrum: treble 'air' and subsonic bass. Traditional tools like equalisation can help bring a degree of professional gloss, but if your kick drum simply hasn't got the low-end power it needs, or that all-important acoustic guitar part has been recorded with a dynamic mic, no amount of strategic equalisation will resolve your problems. Whenever the sonic issues go beyond the capabilities of EQ, it's time to turn to Logic Pro's special branch of plug-ins, and, in particular, the SubBass and Exciter.

Bomb the bass

SubBass, as the name suggests, is a plug-in that can be used to generate additional bass frequencies below that of its input. As with the Exciter, SubBass should only be turned to in those situations where the required harmonic material can't be found in the existing sound. For

WHEN SONIC ISSUES GO BEYOND THE CAPABILITIES OF EQ, TURN TO LOGIC PRO'S SPECIAL BRANCH OF PLUG-INS.

example, suppose you've lifted a kick drum by 60Hz using EQ but found little or no frequency information in that area. Of course, you can use SubBass on any type of material, but the best results are achieved with low-pitched drums such as the kick.

Working on the Kick Drum track in the Tutorial file, load an instance of the SubBass plug-in. The plug-in is actually divided into two frequency-generation sections – High

and Low – which can be found towards the top and bottom of the interface respectively. In terms of generating the required sub-bass, a good starting point is to set the mix between dry and wet versions of the signal – in other words, the original signal and the synthesized component – with a clear bias towards the wet part. This way you'll clearly hear the synthesized sub-bass alongside a touch of the original part. Try settings of 10% dry and 205 wet to begin with. **1**

Woofer shaker

In theory, you can generate two synthesised sub-harmonics with SubBass, but you'll probably find that it's best to stick with just a single generator for most bass-swelling applications. To do this, set the Mix tab to either 0 or 100, so that you hear only one of the relevant section's controls.

The plug-in's three primary parameters are Ratio, Centre and Bandwidth – with Ratio governing the tuning of the effect (a setting of 2, for example, places the frequency an octave below source), while Centre and Bandwidth enable you to focus the SubBass analysis engine on a specific part of the sound. **2**

In the example of our kick, try to tune in the frequency until you find a setting that complements the existing fundamental pitch of the kick drum – in this case, around 80Hz. In situations where the original material is relatively fixed in pitch, keep the Bandwidth relatively narrow – no more than 0.2 Oct – so that newly generated harmonics are tightly focused to the original sound.

Instruments with a broader span of pitch, such as a bass guitar, would require a higher Bandwidth setting, though this can lead to a degree of distortion becoming evident in the signal. In the final mix, restore the balance of the dry input to 100% and then mix in the wet component as desired. **3**

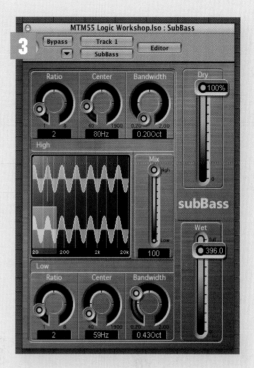

Logic Pro's SubBass and Exciter plug-ins are both excellent ways of adding harmonic information that EQ alone cannot provide. Tune their parameters carefully, though, to ensure that the results are both tasteful and sonically effective.

Pure Excitement

In contrast to SubBass, the Exciter plug-in generates new harmonic material at the top end of the audio spectrum. Again, the Exciter is something to turn to when EQ fails, especially in the region of 12kHz and above – also known as 'air' – which can sometimes become lost in the process of recording. The Exciter works in a similar way to the Aphex Aural Exciter; it takes a high-pass filtered version of the signal, distorts it – adding harmonic information – and then mixes it back into the original input. You can see this process in action by looking at the interface's display, which illustrates the high-pass filter and its associated Frequency parameter.

Now let's experiment with the Overheads track, and attempt to introduce air to the signal. The main two parameters are Frequency and Harmonics. When setting the Frequency parameter, try to find a position somewhere towards the top of the existing audio spectrum – a setting that's too low will make the result unnatural, so in this case opt for around 7,900Hz. The Harmonics control might be better described as a mix control, specifying the amount of distorted signal – and extra harmonic information – blended with the input. Tools such as these are extremely addictive and it's easy to overcook, so try to find a percentage that adds a little sparkle but that doesn't sound deliberately pushed.

The Exciter's other parameters are its two Color settings – Color 1 and Color 2. Essentially, these vary the drive and tone of the distortion produced, with Color 1 offering a more subtle tone and Color 2 adding a greater amount of harmonic material.

Buss-powered

Although we've explored both effects in the context of individual sounds, there's no reason why you can't apply them across a buss – adding excitement to a percussion subgroup, for example – or even across the entire mix. The trick is to keep the use of SubBass and Exciter as the exception rather than the rule, reserving them for those hopefully rare moments where conventional wisdom and traditional studio processing can't deliver the results and 'hype' you're looking for.

Power Tip

The Exciter's Input control is a superb way to monitor the exact timbre of the frequencies you're adding through the process of excitation. By unchecking the Input control, you hear only the high-pass filtered material and none of the original source. This enables you to set the frequency point in a more informed way, as you're hearing only the added component. It's also an excellent way to gauge exactly how much excitement you want to blend back into the mix.

"I did a session with Tuff Jam at a studio in East London somewhere and they had one of the first versions of Logic…"

MARK YARDLEY, STANTON WARRIORS

MusicTech INTERVIEW
Stanton Warriors

Stanton Warriors are one of the UK's leading breaks producers, famed around the world for their storming DJ sets, high-profile remixes and collaborations. The duo's Mark Yardley talks tech and explains how Logic became their software of choice.

Dominic Butler and Mark Yardley are Stanton Warriors, the formidable breakbeat duo who have been producing, DJ-ing and remixing for over a decade. They have become known for their Stanton Sessions DJ sets and for the identically named compilation albums that feature the duo's own productions alongside the best artists the scene has to offer. They have also become associated with clubs like Fabric, contributing number 30 in the well-regarded *Fabric Live* series. They have collaborated with some of the biggest names, including Rodney P and Sway, and remixed a whole bunch more, including Fatboy Slim, Missy Elliot and Basement Jaxx. In 2006 they became the first breaks act to sign to a major, releasing their debut artist album *Lost Files* through V2. Over the years they have picked up just about every dance award going. We caught up with Mark Yardley as he looked back at ten years of music production.

"When I started out as a programmer and engineer, I used to be a Cubase guy," he says. "This was back in the days of the MIDI-only Atari ST, when if you wanted to record vocals you sync'ed it to a 24-track reel-to-reel, or flew them in off an Akai sampler. One day I did a session with Tuff Jam at a studio in East London somewhere and they had one of the first versions of Logic and hard disk recording. I was pretty much hooked after that session."

Mark started seeing Logic in many of the studios he worked in. "It was fast becoming an industry standard so

the choice was kind of made for me," he recalls. "It was the way it combined working with hard disk audio and MIDI – which was still a huge part of the process before the age of software samplers and instruments – that made it the sequencer of choice for studios focused round dance production. I used Cubase Audio and VST occasionally when clients had sessions started on it, but it never had the same ergonomics that Logic had – it seemed kind of clunky in comparison."

Nowadays Mark has the latest version of Logic, which does, of course, now boast all the software instruments, samplers and effects he mentions. As the power of the software has increased, so has Logic's importance within the Warriors' studio.

Outboard gear
"Logic 8 is the hub of our setup," Mark confirms. "We always seem to be working on loads of different projects at the same time. I still use a fair bit of outboard gear and having total recall on mixes is key, so all our outboard comes up in Logic as plugs so I can switch between mixes without loads of repatching. We still use the [E-mu] SP1200 and the [Akai] MPC for beats but they always come back into Logic as audio for mixing."

Stanton Warriors are famed for their live-remix DJ sets, where they take apart and re-imagine tracks, beats and mixes, throwing all sorts of styles, genres and ingredients in. When they first started DJ-ing their sets needed some pretty heavy machinery, until Logic came along… ▶

SELECTED KIT LIST
- Apple Mac running Logic 8
- Ableton Live
- Akai MPC
- E-mu SP1200
- Evolution UC-33e
- M-Audio FireWire 410
- M-Audio Oxygen 8
- M-Audio MicroTrack 2 recorder
- M-Audio Trigger Finger

1 Mark has recently converted his entire breaks collection into Apple Loops. He can now audition his collection within Logic, knowing they will play at the correct tempo. To convert breaks into Apple Loops, first open your arrangement and import a break. The break we have chosen here has a tempo of 80bpm but the project tempo is 107bpm. Click on the Audio dropdown menu and open the file with the Open In Apple Loops Utility option.

2 The next dialogue offers you a choice on how to fit your loop to the bars and beats in Logic. You can increase it to a set length or decrease it to the nearest bar. We chose the latter option. The next dialogue after that asks you to provide information about how the loop sounds and some other characteristics, like effect processing and time signature. Put as much information as you can in here as it helps tag the file for future searches.

3 Click on Looping and input the tempo of the original file. Saving out here should result in your break being converted to a perfect Apple Loop that matches the tempo of your song. If you are not happy you can adjust the Transient sensitivity in the Transient tag. It's the top slider and you can check the results by changing the tempo at the bottom. Save out when you are happy. Now experiment with Matrix modulation on everything!

"When we first did live-remix DJ sets back in the late 90s (filtering and chopping acapellas and sound effects over beats), using a laptop for triggering audio in a club just wasn't an option. I used to carry around an Akai S3200XL with 32MB RAM, flight-cased with a Zip drive and triggered via a Novation BassStation, which was the smallest keyboard you could get. Around 2000, I switched to a Mac laptop running Logic and used the EXS24 instead of the Akai to cut down on the chiropractor bills!"

That setup has been superseded by Ableton Live and some M-Audio controllers, but Logic still has its place in the Stanton studio, even if it doesn't dictate the way they make music. So what features within Logic 8 get used the most when the Stantons are in production mode?

"The new Multiple Take feature when you loop and record is great," Mark replies. "It makes organising mammoth vocal sessions much easier. I'm using channel strips more these days for recalling lengthy plug-in chains. Since I converted my entire break collection to Apple Loops last year, I'm enjoying the immediacy of quick loop auditioning within Logic, rather than always having to boot and rewire Live. The Apple Loop manipulation is rarely what I'm after but I can get an idea going and port it out to Live, ReCycle, the SP or MPC from there."

But there is one small aspect of the software that Mark thinks could and should be improved:

"It irks me that Logic has always truncated audio file names past 26 characters when loading into Audio Bin. This throws up all sorts of problems with locating audio files that have been used over different projects. Also, when you're exporting breaks from ReCycle, which adds numerical identifiers at the end of the sample name (.001, .002, etc) this pushes the character count over 26. Now when you import slices into Audio Bin, Logic truncates the number and sticks some random number at the end. I think it's been that way since OS9. Surely we don't have to put up with limitations on the size of the title of an audio file when such advances have been made elsewhere!"

That said, Mark has noted improvements in the latest version: "The automation now feels up to scratch," he says. "So far I haven't noticed any of the glitchy behaviour I used to get in version 7. The suite of Logic plug-ins

> "The Apple Loop manipulation is rarely what I'm after, but I can get an idea going and port it out." **MARK YARDLEY**

houses a lot of power and the little tweaks and additional features have improved them further. The Sidechain filter and Mix control on the Compressor is a great addition. The multi-take recording is great and Quick Swipe comping is really helping to speed up our recording."

Mark and Dominic are as busy as ever this year with remix, DJ and production duties. "We have a new single coming out in August on our label, Punks, which we wrote with rap legend Big Daddy Kane, called *Get Wild*," says Mark. "We're currently working on various remixes, including Toe Jam featuring David Byrne and Dizzee Rascal for Norman Cook's Brighton Port Authority project, and a Plump DJs remix. We are also putting together our *Stanton Sessions Volume 3*, which will be out later in the year and we'll continue doing Stanton Sessions nights at various clubs around the world."

If you want to catch up with the Stantons, visit: www.myspace.com/stantonwarriors and www.stantonwarriors.com **MTF**

Stanton Warriors have a busy schedule of gigs coming up all over the world. Check the MySpace URL at the end of this feature for more info.

Think Inside The Box

Sound Module • Audio Interface • Media Player

The Sonic Cell puts sounds from the legendary Roland Fantom workstations on your desktop. Expand your sonic palette by adding optional SRX boards, and connect to your computer through the built-in USB audio interface. You can even take the Sonic Cell out on the road, as it's capable of playing back audio and MIDI files: perfect for the gigging musician.

Sonic Cell: from the studio to the stage, it's all in the box.

www.roland.co.uk/soniccell or call 0845 1305 909

REASON

MIDI & Audio Hardware Interface

MClass Mastering Suite
Pristine quality EQ, stereo imager,
compressor and maximizer

reMix 14:2 14 Channel Stereo Mixer

RV7000 Advanced Reverb

Thor Polysonic Synthesizer
Semi modular synth with 6 high quality
oscillator types, 4 filter units, analog
sequencer, flexible control and routing

Redrum Drum Computer
Pattern based, 10 channel drum machine

MClass Compressor

Malström Graintable Synthesizer
Unique sound based on granular synthesis

Combinator
The Combinator lets you play and build elaborate
layered instruments and effects by combining
Reason's devices in a rack within the rack

MClass Stereo Imager

Subtractor Analog Synthesizer
Dual oscillator, dual filter analog synth

PH-90 Phaser & UN-16 Unison Effects

Matrix Pattern Sequencer
Control voltage step sequencer

NN-XT Advanced Sampler
Fully featured professional sampler

MClass EQ
Two parametric & two shelving bands

Dr.Rex Loop Player, Plays REX loops from
Reason's sound library or loops created with ReCycle

Scream 4 Sound Destruction Unit
Multimode distortion device

ECF-42 Envelope Controlled Filter & PEQ-2 Two Band EQ

Thor with programmer folded in

Comp-01 Compressor/Limiter

RPG-8 Monophonic Arpeggiator

Combinator with the programmer folded in

BV-512 Digital Vocoder with 4 to 512 bands

DDL-1 Digital Delay & CF-101 Chorus/Flanger

Subtractor Analog Synthesizer

UN-16 Unison & DDL-1 Digital Delay

NN-19 Digital Sampler

RV7000 Advanced Reverb

ReGroove Groove Mixer
Real-time, hands on control over all your groove settings

Built in the shape of a classic studio rack,
Reason is an all-in-one production
environment containing all the gear you
possibly need: samplers, analogue synths,
graintable synth, vocoder, mixer, step time
drum machine, arpeggiator, compressors,
EQ and effects - everything you need to
turn good ideas into full-blown
productions.

Used stand-alone, or connected
to your existing software via
ReWire, Reason is an
indespensible musical tool.

REWIRE

ReWire compatible hosts include Live, Logic, ProTools,
Digital Performer and Cubase.

For more information please visit
www.propellerheads.se and
www.soundtech.co.uk/propellerhead

propellerhead

Programming sounds in Sculpture

Of all Logic Pro 8's instruments, Sculpture is perhaps the most untapped. Mo Volans demystifies the challenging interface of one of the best synths in your collection.

An inspection of most of the synths supplied with Logic 8 will reveal a good range of virtual analogue and subtractive-based designs. Yet though these instruments provide good sonic flexibility and great sound quality, they are all very similar beasts. A single glance over the interface of Sculpture, however, will soon let you know that here you are dealing with something way out of the ordinary.

Sculpture uses component-modelling technology, a sound-creation system that was once limited to high-end workstations and expensive lead synths. Now mostly used for plug-ins designed to re-create classic signal processors, component modelling works by mathematically analysing the characteristics of each part of an instrument or circuit. This process is time consuming for the manufacturer and can be costly in terms of CPU usage for the end user, but it is currently the most accurate way of re-creating real world instruments and machines in virtual form.

In regards to synthesis, component modelling has two areas in which it can be put to good use: virtual analogue modelling and the mimicking of acoustic instruments.

Power Tip

When you're editing sound in the string section, it can be useful to see exactly how your objects are effecting the string and how it is vibrating. If you [Ctrl]-click (or right-click) on the area, an Enable String Animation option will be displayed. Once this is engaged you should see the string moving within the window as you play. Having this visual feedback gives you a real idea of how each object works and can greatly aid your editing.

Sculpture falls into the latter category, in that some of its sections model real-world objects to generate sound. But the real beauty of the instrument is that there is also an option to feed these objects through traditional processors and synthesizer components to twist them beyond recognition. You might say that Sculpture borrows from two areas of synthesis to generate and manipulate sound.

Innovative oscillators

The structure of Sculpture is similar to many synths in that it does have oscillators, but where it differs from the rest is that the oscillators that initially create the sound do not use the usual saw-tooth, square-wave or wavetable formula but a more organic 'string'. This means that the sound of the synth is very different from its counterparts and that it generally sounds much more organic. This system of mixing real-world sounds with traditional synth technologies is hugely flexible and enables you to program anything from an acoustic steel guitar to evolving granular textures – and everything in between.

The real key to Sculpture's overall sound, however, lies in its innovative oscillators. These cleverly mimic ▶

YOU MIGHT SAY SCULPTURE BORROWS FROM TWO AREAS OF SYNTHESIS TO GENERATE AND MANIPULATE SOUND.

objects hitting a string or bar. There are three oscillators – or 'objects', as Sculpture likes to call them. These objects can all play at once and be mixed together to taste. They're called 'objects' because they aren't really oscillators at all, in the strictly traditional sense. A standard synthesizer oscillator is the synth's only sound source and is represented by a wave or sample. Within Sculpture, however, objects are simply actions that generate sound. The actual oscillator is a string represented in the window

THEY'RE CALLED 'OBJECTS' BECAUSE THEY AREN'T REALLY OSCILLATORS AT ALL, IN THE STRICTLY TRADITIONAL SENSE.

located within the three objects. Dropdown menus within the objects enable you to decide whether the string is struck, picked, bowed or blown on – there are also plenty of more diverse options such as gravity strikes, bounces, bounds and noises for unusual effects.

The string itself has options within its window to further control its behaviour. Two pickups, represented by bars, can be moved to drastically change the sound's timbre and character. Among the other controls featured are the object position sliders, which are represented by large sliders with corresponding numbers. Having the

ability to decide exactly where on the string each action or object occurs gives you a huge amount of control over the sound that is finally produced. A good session of experimentation with different combinations of these parameters will be invaluable in helping you to become familiar with them.

Material pad

The central and possibly most important part of Sculpture's interface is the Material Pad. Here you can select what material the string is constructed from and even morph between materials in real time.

The pad works in much the same way as the X/Y vector control found on many larger synths and control surfaces. The moving 'ball' acts as a mixer control, so you can achieve any number of combinations between the different materials. Things get really interesting when you learn that this parameter can also be automated.

Along with the options to create glass, steel, wood or nylon materials, the pad area also contains controls to adjust resolution and harmonics, media loss and tension modulation. These are all specific properties of a vibrating string and adjustments here will help create a more realistic result (if that's what you're looking for). The way these parameters are viewed can also be changed by large buttons in the lower section of the material pad.

Placed directly after the objects and material pad is a

STEP-BY-STEP   Creating varying sounds using the string.

1 Select your objects and decide what you want them to do. This example shows a clavichord-like sound being constructed, so the string is struck. The first object provides basic actions; the more unusual actions are contained within objects 2 and 3.

2 Move to the string display and move the object sliders until you are happy with the sound. The display shows a virtual bridge to the left and a neck can be imagined to the right. Moving the objects to either side will make radically different sounds.

3 Now move the pickup markers – these are also shown in the string section. These have a pretty extreme effect too. Moving the markers to the far left or right will result in thinner sounds; anything towards the centre will sound warmer, with richer harmonics.

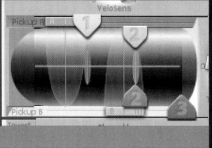

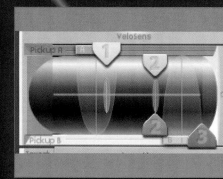

4 Choose the material of your instrument's string. A harsh, steel-based sound is used here; nylon or wood create a much warmer, more resonant sound. Different materials have different dynamic characteristics; these can be fine-tuned with the controls around the pad.

5 Adjust the resolution, media loss and tension mod controls to tailor the sound to your liking. If you need guidance, you can always change the display mode to show guidelines while you're editing your sound. Key-scale and release modes are available here.

6 Finally, add any voice-based effects you feel you need. We've added some basic vibrato to provide interest and to give the new instrument a more realistic, human feel. Note that many of Sculpture's modulators and effects can be synced to Logic's bpm.

SOME FEATURES OF THE INSTRUMENT HAVE OBVIOUSLY BEEN DESIGNED FOR USE HERE ONLY.

Power Tip

If you feel that your new sound has turned out a little clean and cold, you could try adding some extra grit to the mix by using the Waveshaper feature. You will find this just above the Material Pad; you activate it with the large button right at the very top of Sculpture's interface. There are several different models to choose from here, from subtle saturation to full-on distortions and overdrives. This can be a great effect for guitar-based presets.

...series of familiar synthesis sections. Anyone remotely familiar with synthesizers will instantly recognise the multi-mode resonant filter, envelopes, LFO sections and effects processors. Using these features you can transform your vibrating string into a synth effect, or perform something as basic as adding release to the sound.

Then there are the other controls that you would expect to be present on any performance synth, such as voice modes, glide controls, transpose, tuning and a warmth control to add a slight analogue-style saturation. Everything you need to make your sound a playable performance instrument is present and correct.

Pretty alien

There are further areas of Sculpture that may well seem pretty alien at first glance. Some features of the instrument have obviously been designed for use here and here only, and are truly bespoke. For example, the morphing controls in the lower area of the synth enable you to morph between many parameters in real time, record your actions and play them back using totally customised patterns. Further to the right a modulation envelope can transform MIDI input into envelope data to modulate various user-defined sources.

Along with jitter, vibrato and external modulation controls, this collection of modulation features make up a true powerhouse of a synthesizer, one that is capable not only of generating sounds like no other but that can also twist these sounds up with almost limitless possibilities.

To put the icing on the cake, Sculpture packs in several processors you can use to polish your sounds. A full stereo delay with dedicated filters and width control is coupled with a Body EQ unit and a master limiter to avoid overloads. With all these tools you will be able to make even the most basic sound shine. MTF

STEP-BY-STEP Polishing your sound with synthesis and effects.

1 To open up your new sound and give it some extra depth, try experimenting with the stereo delay processor included with Sculpture. This has built-in hi- and low-pass filters and an editing pad to strike a balance between stereo depth and groove.

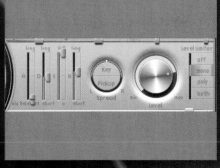

2 Adjust the amplitude envelope to achieve the sound you want. Here, some release was added to make the string ring out after it had been struck – this makes the sound much more playable and realistic. You can also input pickup spread and limiter settings here.

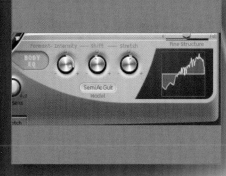

3 Some EQ can do wonders to your sound. Sculpture's Body EQ has some great presets that use actual models of instruments to modify the sound. These models can then be tweaked once they're loaded or, if you prefer, you can stick to more traditional EQ.

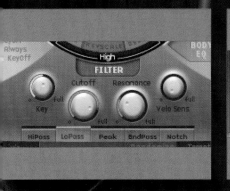

4 Move to the filter section and activate it by hitting the large Filter button. Choose one of the five modes and add some resonance if needed. A sensible filter setting can enhance your sound a great deal; more extreme amounts will transform the instrument completely.

5 If you feel you would like some extra movement in the filter section, you can always employ an LFO for the task. Subtle settings here can bring the sound to life, adding dynamics and making the sound breathe. The LFOs are both fully syncable to Logic's clock.

6 A second LFO modulating one of the more obscure sources can add an extra dimension. Here you can see that a slow, synced waveform is used to modulate some pan settings – a very subtle but pleasant effect, not unlike when an auto-panner is added.

the perfect mix...

...of form and function

The new MC Control brings the unparalleled speed, resolution and DAW integration of Euphonix' high-end professional consoles to your studio in a revolutionary, slim-line design. The high-resolution, customizable touchscreen and ergonomic controls let you effortlessly navigate and edit your projects without ever touching a mouse, and place everything from simple keystroke commands to complex custom macros at your fingertips to deliver an unmatched editing and mixing experience.

musikmesse international press award **m.i.p.a.**
Best Recording Hardware winner 2008

reddot design award winner 2008

euphonix.com

MusicTech
INTERVIEW
Slam

Slam have made music with just about every combination of hardware and software you can think of. But their hardware collection is under threat as Logic takes over.

Slam have been producing their unique blend of techno since the early 90s – and they have the kit list to prove it! Orde Meikle and Stuart McMillan also have their own label, Soma Records, with artists like Black Dog and Silicone Soul, and they run several high-profile events, from their own Slam Tent at T In The Park to monthly Pressure parties in their home city of Glasgow. But it's always been music-making at the heart of it all and their approach to it is to, well, not have an approach.

"It's changed so much over the years," says Orde. "It's very liquid with no rules – whatever, wherever, whenever – but lots of hours. We've found our best stuff comes very quickly. One idea spurns another and the jigsaw just fits into place in a couple of hours – then the fine-tuning takes days. Embracing new technology is something we're passionate about; not getting caught in the old engineer's rut where you think you know how every sound is made. It's the ones you've never heard before that we're after. That's electronica: it's music you've only dreamed of."

And embrace technology is something Slam certainly have done. As we've mentioned, and as you can see, they do have quite a kit list, but at its core Logic controls, sequences, records and arranges everything. And it's been this way for some time now:

"We used Steinberg Cubase since the Atari days – black and white screens and only four MIDI outs," recalls

SELECTED KIT LIST

- Apple Mac G5 with twin screens running Logic and Live
- Trident Desk
- Dynaudio BM6A
- Genelec 1080
- Klein and Hummel O300
- Sony SRS-Z1 and Yamaha NS10m monitors
- Korg Micro Kontrol
- Logic Control
- M-Audio O2 keyboards
- M-Audio FireWire 410
- SE Reflexion Filter
- TC Powercore
- Tons of plug-ins!
- Tons (literally) of hardware synths (25 at last count) and samplers
- Yamaha Tenori-on

Orde. "Then we moved to Macs very early when they weren't powerful at all. We discovered Logic when we decided to use an engineer to produce our first album, *Headstates*. We arrived with lots of DATs with audio takes and MIDI files on floppy discs. He was using a very early version of Logic, which was then produced by Emagic. We haven't looked back since. The more we used it the better it got and slowly everyone else we knew started using it. It's almost become an industry standard."

Dramatic introduction

That sounds like quite a dramatic introduction. So what was it that drew them in so quickly?

"God, where do you start?" says Orde. "At first it was the tightness of Logic that attracted us. As we dug deeper it was the flexibility of the MIDI environment. The user interface was just so well thought out and the quality of the audio was exceptional for those days. The onboard effects were good – not the best – but still very good. When they started to produce things like the early plug-in synths, vocoder and the EXS24, with great samples you would have to pay extra for with any other sequencer, it just became an indispensable part of the way we worked. It just is the daddy!"

Slam have seen – as we all have – a massive shift from using hardware to going software-only. But for them, with these amounts of hardware, the shift has been seismic, as Orde details:

▶

 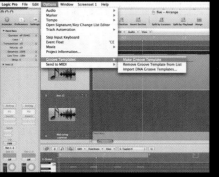 

1 One of Orde's top tips was to spend time setting up template pages. We've covered that with Bombay Monkey but another of his specific favourites was to include your own groove quantizes in such a template. This is a very useful feature in Logic that enables you to set up quantization types based on grooves in other MIDI parts. First of all, select a region that has interesting nuances that you want to apply elsewhere.

2 Two-bar regions work best, though you can use a part of any length. Go to the Options menu and choose Groove Templates>Make Groove Template. The groove characteristics of your selected part will be copied to the Groove menu above the Piano Roll Edit page.

3 Our original part was called Hard Bass and you can see that the Groove template of this has now appeared in the Groove menu. If you want to use this on another part's notes, select that part, pull down to the Hard Bass option in this menu and all the timings will be copied. This is a great option if you have (possibly even accidentally!) come up with an intricate timing that you want to keep. Save the project out as a Template and your new Groove template will be stored for future use.

▶ "In the studio it's our workhorse. We used to run so much live at first with 24 MIDI channels plus some audio all running onto DAT. But as hard disk space got cheaper the MIDI side of our Logic setup got used less and less. It was a case of a lot of automation and multiple takes with live tweaking bouncing it all into audio and then editing that. Now we hardly leave the Mac; we do everything inside the box – the onslaught of software has been incredible! Sometimes we'll bring certain stems through

"There hasn't been anything come onto the market that's made us think about swapping to another

our desk and outboard or turn on an old bit of hardware but, to be fair, it isn't that often now. Even our much-loved Apogee is used mostly for monitoring now. The quality of the digital domain is just fantastic: effects, keyboards, drum machines… the list is endless."

Yet while Logic has taken over in the studio, on the road it's a different story: "We don't use Logic live, though I've heard MainStage is good," says Orde. Live, Slam use Ableton Live controlled by M-Audio O2 keyboards, which they also use with Logic in the studio.

You'll recall our mentioning the extensive list of hardware Slam have built up over the years? Looks pretty impressive, doesn't it?

"We've been using Logic for so long now it just is the way we work. As the program has changed, so we have changed. There hasn't been anything come onto the market that's made us think about swapping to another sequencer. Most people we know use Apple Macs and therefore Logic. It's got everything you need. Some bits may not be top of the digital tree but they're mostly pretty good and at the price it's incredible."

Nothing is perfect
So is there anything that they'd like to see added in future versions? "Nothing is perfect and that's what updates are all about," replies Orde. "To be fair, the programmers do seem to be listening to the forums and they do encourage user-interaction to solve problems and add features. But they're not always fast enough, preferring to drip-feed improvements – cash-generating, I'm sure."

"A couple of things that would make Logic better for us," he continues, "would be the ability to record audio/bounce and replace or drop the new file automatically onto a new track below the original [sounds like this could be dealt with by the new Comping feature in v8 – Ed]. Bouncing multiple outs simultaneously would be cool, as would display and manipulation of freeze files.

"The ability to export audio files with all automation data would be good, as would the ability to show all personalised grooves on the Autoload page. There are probably a few more things, but we don't want to moan!"

So after years of using Logic, Slam must have some top tips on how to get the best from it. Yes, indeed!

"Set up key commands to speed up your workflow," says Orde. "Set up an Autoload page [Template] with your own groove quantizes. Back up and back up again!"

"For us a mixture of good ideas and happy accidents in the studio are always the most fruitful. Interaction with other producers is important, and reading magazines is a fantastic way to learn – never stop learning!"

Slam are setting up a new label called Paragraph and are just finalising the first releases. They are also about to embark on a big studio overhaul, including a 're-tweak' of the acoustics, and then take a much needed holiday. "No laptop for two weeks," laughs Orde. **MTF**

Genelec studio monitoring.
Now available on your desktop.

If you're a recording professional, chances are your studio monitors are made by Genelec. Now the new 6010A active speakers and optional 5040A subwoofer deliver 35Hz - 18kHz of Genelec reference-quality studio monitoring to your desktop – perfect for DAW production, mobile recording, audio editing and your iPod.

Get Genelec studio monitoring for your desktop. Discover the 6010A and 5040A at your nearest Genelec dealer.

GENELEC®

www.genelec.com/firststep

Number one by design.

INTRODUCING
The Studiophile BX Deluxe Series

What happens when you surpass what people expect from a near-field reference monitor? You end up with the USA's best selling* monitor in its category—the M-Audio Studiophile™ BX5a. Now our obsession with perfection has led us to raise the bar again. Meet the Studiophile BX5a Deluxe and the Studiophile BX8a Deluxe. The BX Deluxe monitors sound balanced at a wide range of volumes, so your mixes will translate across diverse listening environments. They also provide detailed sonic imaging, seamless frequency integration and an amazingly cohesive sound. The BX Deluxe monitors are designed to deliver an exceptional monitoring experience that's true to your music. Hear for yourself at your local M-Audio dealer.

Source: MI SalesTrak

> GET M-POWERED

Studiophile BX5a Deluxe

- 70 watts of bi-amped power
- 5" Kevlar low-frequency drivers
- 1" natural silk high-frequency drivers
- XLR balanced and 1/4" TRS inputs
- Optimage IV wave guides

Studiophile BX8a Deluxe

- 130 watts of bi-amped power
- 8" Kevlar low-frequency drivers
- 1-1/4" natural silk high-frequency drivers
- XLR balanced and 1/4" TRS inputs
- Optimage IV wave guides

To learn more about M-Audio's complete line of monitors, please visit *www.maudio.co.uk/monitors*.

M-AUDIO® | 20 years

www.maudio.co.uk

LOGIC PRO 8 WORKSHOP

LOGIC'S ENVIRONMENT

Despite first appearances, the concepts behind Logic's Environment are easy to grasp and put to good use. **Mark Cousins** campaigns for a better environment.

Ask people what scares them most about Logic and you can almost guarantee that you'll get the same answer from everyone: the Environment. This is a shame, because it needn't be this way. Once you understand what the Environment is actually there to do, much of its mystery will be revealed and you will feel much more comfortable working within it. This, in turn, will bring you great benefits in the form of improved Logic productions.

Most of the confusion people have about the Environment seems to stem from some general, basic misunderstandings about its role. Is it the glue that binds Logic together? Is it nothing more than an archaic throwback to the days of MIDI? Or is it just a means of perplexing new users? It is, of course, the former, though that answer in itself will not be enough to assuage many people's fears. So let us continue.

In truth, the Environment's role has now become sidelined from the everyday use of Logic – largely as a result of Apple's attempts to simplify the operation of the application and make it more accessible – but it's still there and for the more creative and experimental user it represents the true heart of Logic's wonderful flexibility

BENEATH LOGIC'S SHINY NEW EXTERIOR IT IS STILL THE ENVIRONMENT THAT KNITS THE APPLICATION TOGETHER.

and charm. It is also the source of some powerful sequencing tools.

There is a lot to learn, and the level to which you try to understand and use the Environment is, of course, up to you. But a rudimentary knowledge will at least enable you to better integrate MIDI hardware into your setup, and give you a better understanding of the path data takes in and out of the sequencer. For the more advanced user, anything is possible – from the creative manipulation of MIDI data using transformers, arpeggiators and so on, through to custom-built editors for hardware synths.

The concept

The Environment was originally designed as a modular solution for routing MIDI data in and out of Logic and designing a virtual representation of your MIDI studio. However, the use of dedicated MIDI hardware is less common these days, which arguably negates the real need for certain elements of the Environment's

Power Tip

With some simple connections you can build your own layering patches from elements of different software instruments. Create a new instrument object and route this through to two or more software instruments. (Logic will ask you to remove the current port assignments, which is fine.) To access the layer effect, drag the newly created instrument object onto the track list and play the layered patch directly from your MIDI keyboard.

functionality. Yet beneath Logic's shiny new exterior it is still the Environment that knits the application together and makes it work. The modular concept may seem complicated but there are plenty of other audio applications that use a similar principle of modules (or objects) strung together with patch cables to make them work – Propellerhead's Reason and Native Instruments' Reaktor are two examples.

The best way to understand the Environment is to start exploring it, and in particular, to see how it has been configured as part of an initialised project. This is what we shall do now. The Environment is accessible from its own window, which can be selected via the keyboard shortcut [Apple+8]. ■

Layer cake

Rather than presenting you with the entirety of the Environment in one go, Logic divides the setup into a series of functional layers, some pre-assembled by Logic, others that can be customised. The first of these layers is the Mixer layer, which presents the audio objects – audio track, metronome, outputs, master faders and so on – that are contained in your session. As you create new tracks, or auxiliary sends, the Mixer layer is updated accordingly. Obviously, the Mixer layer replicates much of what the Mixer pane in the Arrange window does, though within the Environment you can see the objects in your audio system in their full glory, even down to aspects like the click and the pre-listen channel. ■

Another important layer is the MIDI Instr layer, which also updates as MIDI tracks are added to your project – though if you've got a number of hardware instruments it often makes more sense to create the desired number of objects for each synth in your collection and then save the project as a project template; this way, whenever you start a new project (using the project template) your MIDI hardware will be pre-assigned and ready for action. ■

Power Tip

Although presets are not usually the ideal way to perfect your plug-in settings, Logic does supply some excellent mastering suites. These pre-constructed chains of plug-ins are available via the Channel Strip menu of the master channel. They aren't a one-stop solution, but they will provide a good starting point for creating a successful mastering setup. Also try calling up presets within the individual plug-ins – some feature dedicated mastering settings.

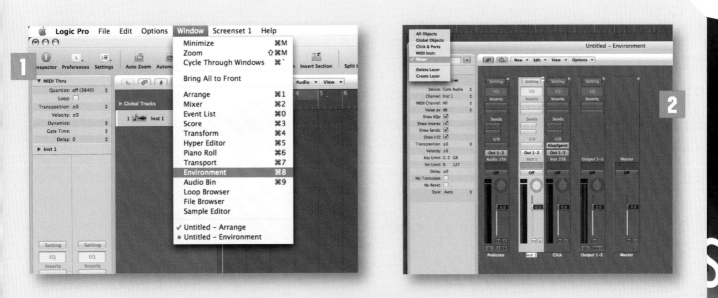

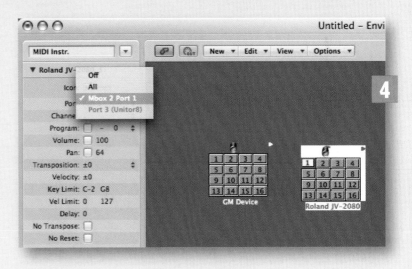

The Environment contains a number of different layers, including the Mixer and the MIDI instrument layers. One rudimentary application of the Environment is to set up and configure a template with all your MIDI hardware pre-assigned to its respective port and MIDI channels.

You can create new instruments in the MIDI Instr layer with the menu commands New>Instrument and New> Multi Instrument. Obviously, the difference between these two object types is the ability to work over 16 MIDI channels – if you're using a multi-timbral workstation, for example – or over a single, assigned MIDI channel in the case of a standard instrument object. After you've put in the appropriate instrument, simply click on the object in question to bring up the Parameter box (on the left side of the Environment window) and define the object's key parameters, such the instrument's name, its MIDI channel, and its port assignment. **4**

Another labour-saving feature of the Multi Instrument object is the ability to select patches by name. Though Logic won't directly import the patch list from the synth, it will enable you to cut and paste a text file – maybe from the manufacturer's patch list, for example; or you could use a patch librarian, such Emagic's old SoundDiver application (available from http://www.apple.com/support/emagic) to interrogate the synth for you. We've also included a collection of multi-instruments with patch names on the *MTF* DVD so you can drag and drop the corresponding multi-instrument into your project. **5**

Click & Ports

Although useful, the Mixer and MIDI Instr layers don't really significantly add to the creative functions and possibilities within Logic. Things get far more interesting, however, when we turn to the Click & Ports layer.

In essence, there are two principle 'routes', or connection paths, within Logic: the route into the sequencer; and the route out of Logic to the instrument, be it virtual or real. The Click & Ports layer shows you the route into Logic from the physical input – in other words, your MIDI input – to the sequencer input. **6**

Looking more closely at the input path you'll notice two objects: a keyboard labelled as Input Notes; and a monitor labelled as Input View. These are connected via a thin grey line – the patchcord – from small node points at the top right corner of the object. Inserted into the input signal path in this way, the two objects work as input

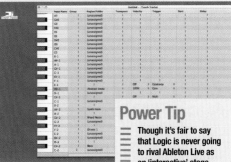

Power Tip

Though it's fair to say that Logic is never going to rival Ableton Live as an 'interactive' stage sequencer, you can achieve 'live' sequencing effects with the Environment's Touch Track object. A touch track maps collection regions from within a project to keys on your MIDI keyboard. Various latching playback modes enable you to build up the mix, region by region, by activating the regions from your MIDI keyboard.

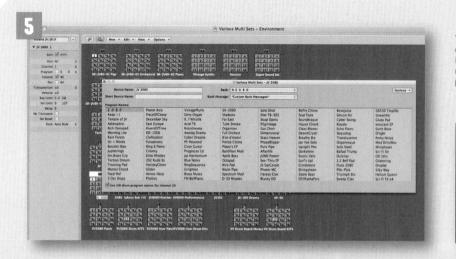

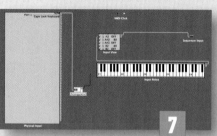

The Arpeggiator is one of the Environment's most exciting creative tools. It is also one of the easiest to use. You can insert the Arpeggiator into the input path – to have the notes recorded into the sequencer – or you can insert it as part of the output path directly into the instrument.

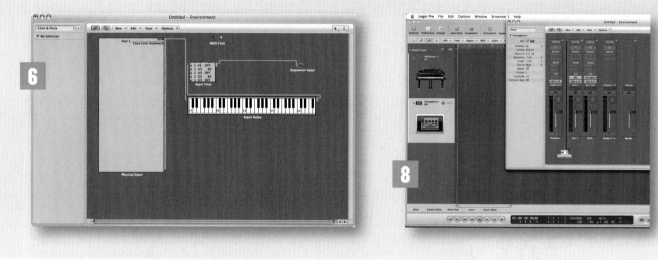

▶ monitors – the keyboard displays the notes played on your controller keyboard, the monitor displays the raw MIDI data that is entering Logic.

One simple, but highly effective, modification of this setup is to insert an arpeggiator into the signal path so Logic arpeggiates the notes you play on the keyboard. To do this, select New>Arpeggiator and re-patch the lead between the physical input and the keyboard so the output of the physical input is connected to the left side of the arpeggiator and from there onto the input of the keyboard. Assuming you have Logic's transport in Play mode, the arpeggiator object should now arpeggiate the input, using the settings 1/8 resolution and so on, defined in the object's parameters. **7**

Outputs

Having looked at the input path, let's turn our attention to the output path. Each instrument in the MIDI Instr layer has a port assignment. These are, in effect, the outputs. Any track assigned to a given object in the arrangement is routed to the appropriate physical output. Likewise, audio tracks in the Arrange window are routed through to accompanying audio objects, as are MIDI tracks to virtual instruments. None of this is rocket science, but what it does mean is that we have the potential to interrupt these typical paths – modifying MIDI data on the way out of Logic, either to external MIDI hardware or to software

instruments in the audio engine, in the same way that we modified data coming in.

Going back to the arpeggiator example, we could wire in the arpeggiator after the output of Logic's sequencer, so that notes are arpeggiated post-sequencer. First, we would need to create an arpeggiator on the mixer layer – you might want to label this so you're clear of its purpose – and then we would route this through to the mixer channel for our virtual instrument. You'll need to direct your sequence data to the arpeggiator, rather than directly to the instrument. You can do this by dragging the arpeggiator object directly over from the Environment to the corresponding track in the Arrange area. **8**

Instrument editors

Another interesting adaptation of the Environment is the design of instrument editors for MIDI hardware, typically using MIDI continuous controller data to modify aspects like filter cutoff and so on. The dilemma here is whether we place our editor objects – which will be in the form of faders – on the input path or on the output path. Ideally, it would be good to be able to record fader moves, in which case we would have to place them on the input path, possibly on the Click & Ports layer. But then it would also be good to see these moves played back, for which we would need to place them on the output path.

The answer to this dilemma (which actually involves

Power Tip

For more complicated environments with many objects, you might avail yourself of the Macro feature. You can use the menu option New>Macro to lock together a number of environment objects. Interestingly, a macro can be cabled just like any other object, though you do need to create two objects – labelled Macro In and Macro Out – to specify the input and output points for your grouped collection of objects.

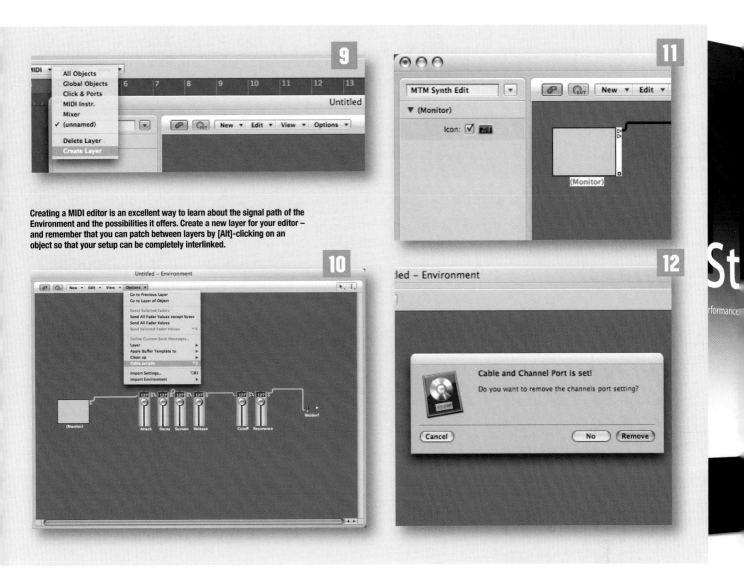

Creating a MIDI editor is an excellent way to learn about the signal path of the Environment and the possibilities it offers. Create a new layer for your editor – and remember that you can patch between layers by [Alt]-clicking on an object so that your setup can be completely interlinked.

using the output path) exploits a little caveat in the specification of the Environment whereby object 'movements' are always recorded onto the currently selected track, irrespective of any cabling. First though, we'll need a layer for our editor – use the Create Layer option under the Layer Selection menu and name the new layer appropriately. 9

The objects required for your editor layer should be a monitor – to view the data entering the layer – followed by a series of faders for each parameter on the synth, and then by an instrument object to create the physical output from the editor, which will need to correspond to the port and channel assignment the instrument is on. With the objects created, you will then need to cable them together, which is easiest to achieve using the function Options>Cable Serially. 10

The final stage is to the route the sequencer's output out through the editor. You could do this by sliding the monitor object you've created onto a spare track lane, but a more elegant alternative – assuming you've already created a physical instrument – is to create a patch between the layers. Before you do this, however, you'll need to click on the monitor object in the editor's layer and make sure its Icon checkbox is enabled, to make it visible in other layers. 11

With this done, move over to the MIDI Instr layer, locate the original instrument and [Alt]-click on its patch

cable point. You are now presented with a menu, split into your existing layers, with the relevant objects selectable. Select your monitor object and Logic will prompt you to remove the port assignments, an action you'll need to confirm by clicking Remove. This seems disconcerting, but all you're actually doing is removing the output point at this stage, in preference to the output later on in the editor's layer. 12

Environmental impact

Though any enthusiastic modifications to the Environment shouldn't be attempted by the faint of heart, you shouldn't ever worry about 'breaking' Logic. The detail can be mind-blowing at times but, as we have just seen, the actual basic concepts that underpin the Environment aren't too hard to grasp and, even if you do fail to achieve the results you are looking for first time, you can always return to the default empty project and start all over again.

That might sound like the perfect recipe for lost time, but your experiments with the Environment might well open up other interesting new ways of working with Logic – and with your studio as a whole. MTF

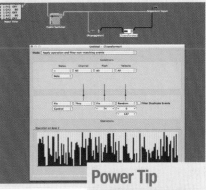

Power Tip

Try experimenting with the various objects in the Environment that can actively manipulate MIDI data – either live, as you play into the Sequencer, or to modify a pre-recorded MIDI part. Two of the best objects to explore are the Arpeggiator (see facing page) and the Transformer. The Transformer is the Environment's version of the Transform editor: it enables you to specify text-based transformations of your MIDI data.

LOGIC PRO 8 WORKSHOP

ON YOUR MusicTech DVD ROM
Full-sized screenshots and all the supporting files you'll need to follow this tutorial.

DELAY DESIGNER

Logic has never been short of delay effects, but Delay Designer goes so much further than anything else. **Mark Cousins** considers some of the uses to which it can be put.

Recording musicians have a wealth of esoteric and exotic effects and plug-ins to choose from, but it's often the most basic tools that are reached for on a daily basis. A prime example is delay – from straightforward slapback treatments on vocals to swirling, rhythmic delays across synths and drums. Indeed, there are few mixes that can't be given an extra dose of flavour or colour by the strategic addition of delay. Of course, Logic Pro has never been short of usable delay effects – check out the marvellous Space Echo-inspired Tape Delay and the Stereo Delay plug-in – but it's Logic Studio's new Delay Designer that's taken delay treatments in Logic Pro to a completely new level.

As the name suggests, Delay Designer enables you to construct your own delay effects using a number of different delay taps, each with its own level, pan, filtering and transposition controls. This degree of flexibility can seem a little daunting at first, but once you've mastered

LOGIC STUDIO'S NEW DELAY DESIGNER TAKES DELAY TREATMENTS IN LOGIC PRO TO A COMPLETELY NEW LEVEL.

Delay Designer you'll have access to a range of unique delay-based effects, many of which are difficult to achieve with other delay plug-ins.

Tap dance
The difference between Delay Designer and the more run-of-the-mill Tape Delay and Stereo Delay is the number of taps – also known as delay lines – available. Tape Delay

has just a single tap and produces basic delay effects; Stereo Delay has two taps, placed to either side of the stereo image, and creates ping-pong-like effects, with the delays bouncing from one side of the soundstage to the other. Delay Designer has a staggering 26 taps, enabling you to custom-build any number of delay effects, from simple slapback to syncopated tempo delays.

One of the best features of Delay Designer is that you can tap in patterns using the Tap Pad to the left of the interface. Working with the instance of Delay Designer on Buss 1 – which is being used to process the drums – try tapping in a short four-step rhythm in time with the drums. Hitting the Start pad initiates the recording, with subsequent hits stored as new tap positions. Click on Last Tap to set your final hit point. Alternatively, just leave Delay Designer to record for its default 10 seconds. The results are displayed in the Tap window. 1

Delay Designer is set to Sync mode by default, which quantizes your taps – labelled A, B, C and D – to neatly defined grid points. You'll probably want to leave the Grid setting as 1/16, with the Swing value set at 50% (no swing), though you can achieve some interesting results by using finer Grid and Swing settings, assuming that the rest of your track has a swing element. Working from your basic pattern, you can alter the placement of the tabs by dragging them to different points on the grid. You can also add new taps or delete existing ones. 2

Delayed reactions
On its own, a static collection of taps doesn't sound particularly interesting. However, manipulate the various settings and the sound becomes significantly more exciting. Although you can see the settings for a selected tap in the Parameter bar across the bottom of the interface, the best way to adjust the settings is to use the Tap Display screen and the Cutoff, Reso, Tansp, Pan and

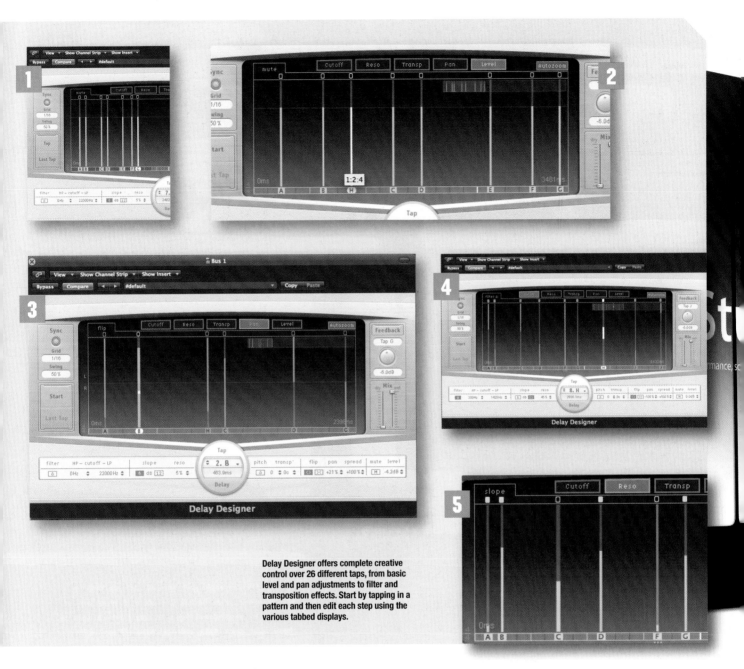

Delay Designer offers complete creative control over 26 different taps, from basic level and pan adjustments to filter and transposition effects. Start by tapping in a pattern and then edit each step using the various tabbed displays.

Level tabs. Try adjusting the levels of each tap, so that each repeat gets progressively quieter. You can also use the Pan tab to bounce the delays around the stereo image, perhaps making the stereo image progressively wider with each repeat. **3**

Some of the most interesting parameters are the Filter settings, which enable you to pass each tap through high- and low-pass filters, and apply varying amounts of resonance. Colouring the delay taps in this way is an important part of getting the results to sit neatly in the mix – if the repeats sound too similar, you'll end up with a cluttered sound, but darker or brighter taps will carve out their own niche in the mix. Unlike the Level controls, notice how each of the filter lines can be dragged from top to bottom, or vice versa, creating low-pass or high- pass filters respectively. Combine both and you can create band-pass filtering effects. **4**

Some of the best applications of the filtering options in Delay Designer come from passing harmonically rich synthesizer sounds through the plug-in. Try experimenting with treatments across the Buzz synth line. You can even

vary the filter slope – between 6dB and 12dB per step – using the Resonance parameters, and you can adjust the transposition of each step. **5**

Unconventional

So far, we've only looked at conventional rhythmic applications for Delay Designer, but you can also achieve plenty of unconventional treatments with the plug-in, such as resonator delays and off-the-wall filtering effects. Most of these effects are achieved through the use of finer grid resolutions – 1/64 or 1/92, for example – and clusters of taps, rather than standard tempo-based divisions. The results you get tend to take on a grainy, metallic edge, with the basic pitch defined by the spacing of the grid – a 64th grid, for example, will sound lower than a 92nd. Adjusting the Filter settings takes this even further, especially when you're using progressive sweeps across extreme settings. **6**

It's also worth remembering that you can combine Delay Designer with Logic's other effects, especially if you're using the plug-in across a buss fader. By keeping ▶

Power Tip

If you've got access to an Apple Remote Control you can use this to remotely operate Logic. You can remotely start and stop the transport, move backwards and forwards bar by bar, and toggle through the various track lanes, all without having to go anywhere near your qwerty keyboard! To record, simply press the Menu button. Remote control makes it far easier to move your microphone away from the noisy fans and hard drives housed in your computer.

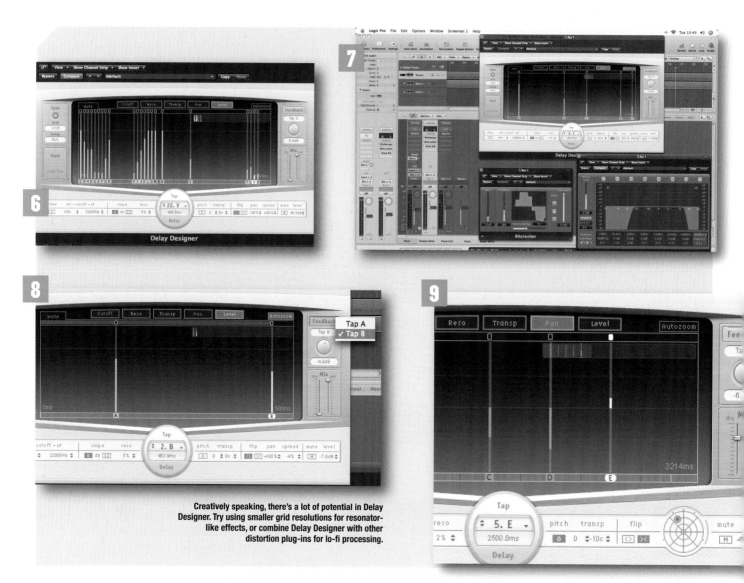

Creatively speaking, there's a lot of potential in Delay Designer. Try using smaller grid resolutions for resonator-like effects, or combine Delay Designer with other distortion plug-ins for lo-fi processing.

THE INCLUSION OF DELAY DESIGNER CAME AT THE SAME TIME AS LOGIC PRO STEPPED UP ITS SURROUND MIXING ABILITIES.

▶ the Delay plug-in away from the original channel, you'll have better control over the timbre of the delays. Assuming you're running the Delay Designer 100% wet, any subsequent plug-ins will modify only the delayed output, leaving your original signal intact at the channel fader. Try adding different distortions to some of the delay effects we've created, including Clip Distortion and BitCrusher for digital grunge, and Dist II for analogue-style treatments. You can also create some interesting sounds by applying an instance of Space Designer. **7**

One of the trickier concepts of Delay Designer is Feedback, which can be found towards the right of the interface. Most delay plug-ins tend to implement this in the form of a simple percentage control that determines the relative amount of delayed signal returned through the delay line. But its implementation in Delay Designer requires you to factor in the tap point – in other words, which of the 26 taps you intend to use as the feedback point. Needless to say, the tap used to generate feedback can have a big effect on the results, both in terms of the

timing of the repeats and, should you use filtering or transposition, their timbre and pitch. A good way of coming to understand this is to use a simple two-tap delay, with each delay panned hard left and right. **8**

Less is more

It's no surprise that the inclusion of Delay Designer came at the same time as Logic Pro seriously stepped up its surround mixing abilities. As a multi-channel plug-in, Delay Designer really comes into its own, enabling you to place a tap anywhere in the surround field. At first, most users tend to get carried away, spinning sounds through 360 degrees, but some of the best effects are achieved through more subtle applications that help to create ambience. Try using short delay times – 40-70ms – on two or three taps positioned in the rear speakers of a 5.1 setup. With a small amount of low-pass filtering at around 8kHz, you should be able to create a delicate amount of rear ambience without resorting to additional reverb. **9**

When it comes to exploring the complete range of effects you can achieve with delay, there are few tools better equipped than Delay Designer. Used correctly, you'll find that delay can help in any number of mixing situations, from simple part thickening to ambience effects and tempo delay. Achieving such a variety of treatments requires a plug-in with significant versatility, which is something that Delay Designer has in spades. **MTF**

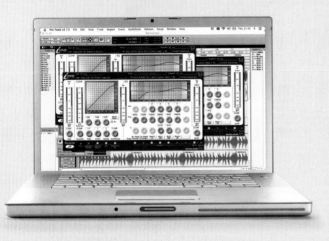

Sidechaining in Logic Pro 8

Logic Pro features native sidechaining out of the box and Apple's implementation of this feature is now seamless. **Mo Volans** shows you how to use it to its full potential.

Sidechaining is currently a very popular topic of conversation among producers and musicians from all genres. A quick glance at any production-orientated internet forum is likely to produce at least a couple of posts about sidechaining technique and the best processors and applications for the job. This could lead one to believe that sidechaining is a new phenomenon introduced by software developers reasonably recently. Nothing could be further from the truth.

Sidechaining has been around for literally decades and has been in the sound engineer's book of tricks for just as long. Many vintage dynamics processors – and plenty of modern ones too – have a 'key input'. This is an input specifically for the purpose of sidechaining and ducking. It is true that this feature has only recently become available in some DAWs, though Logic has had this area covered for some time.

There is a widespread misconception that sidechaining is ducking and vice-versa. This misconception is mainly due to the massive popularity of ducking bass lines in

SIDECHAINING HAS BEEN IN THE SOUND ENGINEER'S BOOK OF TRICKS FOR LITERALLY DECADES.

Power Tip

When you're using sidechain compressors to achieve classic ducking and pumping effects you may get some wayward, rogue transients in the mix. This is sometimes due to large amounts of gain reduction either side of a large transient in your treated sound. You can even things out by applying some limiting directly after your sidechain compressor. Don't apply too much, though, or you will iron out the ducking effect.

some forms of modern music. Many producers see ducking as the only use for sidechaining and tend to overlook its other possible applications – yet ducking itself can be applied to FX busses, vocals and even percussion, and can be much more versatile than you might imagine.

What is a sidechain?

First of all, it's worth looking at what sidechaining actually is. This will help to clarify what it can be used for and how you can implement it within Logic Pro.

A sidechain is essentially a duplicate of an audio stream, routed to a required destination. In most cases, this routed signal is only used to trigger a parameter within the chosen processor; it is usually never actually heard again in the mix. A sidechain, therefore, could best be described as something half way between a send and an insert. ▶

What your sidechained audio does and where it is routed to is, of course, totally up to you. It can be used for many purposes, from reducing gain in a compressor for classic ducking effects to feeding audio to gates and vocoders for more experimental sounds. But whatever you use sidechained audio for, it's useful to remember that absolutely any sound in your mix can be used for the 'source'. Once you have grasped this concept you will realise that you have access to a very powerful routing

TRY APPLYING THE SIDECHAIN COMPRESSOR TO A REVERB BUSS OR A BACKING VOCAL LINE.

matrix between the sounds in your mix and many processors in Logic Pro.

It's well worth checking all the processors that support sidechaining in Logic as some of them may come as a bit of a surprise. You may not have expected to find a sidechain input on the ring modulator or on auto-filter plug-ins, for example.

We will now break down the main plug-ins that accept sidechain inputs into sections and suggest possible ways in which you can utilise them.

Compressing and expanding

These are the most obvious processors when it comes to sidechain capability and probably the most heavily used. If you want to achieve classic ducking and pumping effects these are the plug-ins you will reach for.

Remember, when it comes to ducking, that the bass line doesn't have to be the treated sound. Try applying the sidechain compressor to a reverb buss or a backing vocal line. Equally, the kick drum doesn't have to be the trigger sound. Sometimes it's really effective to duck one guitar line as another plays. This sort of treatment can allow some elements to cut through a busy mix without your having to remove other instruments.

Logic has added plenty of new features to its main compressor in version 8 so it's worth familiarising yourself with these. For instance, on opening the extended controls you will see that there are now distortion settings, frequency-dependent sidechain settings and even a mix control. Also, when choosing your sidechain source – and this goes for all sidechain-capable plug-ins – the channels' names are now displayed for improved workflow.

If you want the opposite effect to ducking, try the Expander. This will enable you to increase the volume by a pre-determined amount and use a sidechain input to trigger the process. This can be extremely useful for creating accents in drum and percussion patterns.

STEP-BY-STEP Setting up a classic ducking effect.

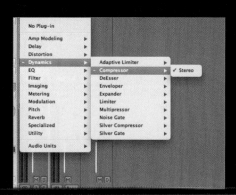

1 First locate the sound you want to trigger your sidechain. I have used a kick drum sample but you could use any sound in your mix. You may find after some experimentation that you get better results using percussive sounds, but every situation is different.

2 Now navigate to the sound you wish to treat with the ducking effect. Again, this can be any sound in your mix, but usually you will focus on a sound that needs to be suppressed to enable other elements to shine. In this case a piano phrase is used.

3 Insert a compressor plug-in on the target channel, making sure that it is of the same format as your sound (mono or stereo). You can now choose the model of compressor you wish to use. Here the platinum model is loaded to ensure maximum transparency.

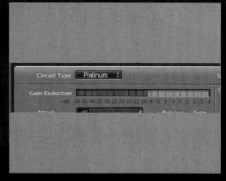

4 Using the dropdown menu Side Chain (in the top right corner of the Compressor's interface), select your trigger sound (the kick drum). This creates the sidechain routing and any compression will now cease. Compression will now only occur if the kick drum is playing.

5 Adjust the attack and release frequencies to complement the program material. Generally, the attack should be pretty fast, while the release will vary from sound to sound and should be adjusted so that it moves in time with your project.

6 Finally, balance the threshold and ratio parameters to reach the desired amount of gain reduction. The further you go the more obvious the effect will be but go too far and the pumping will become so intense that you may lose portions of your sound.

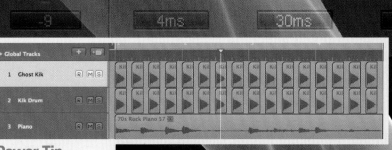

THERE ARE SOME PLUG-INS YOU MAY NOT EXPECT TO ACCEPT SIDECHAIN SIGNAL AT ALL, BUT THEY DO.

Noise gates

Noise gates may not be the first type of processor you think of when it comes to sidechaining but in fact some of the most creative results can come from these unassuming little plug-ins. You may have seen groove-based gates on synthesizers and other instruments… Well now you can create the same effects on any audio, with any groove.

When the gate's side input is activated it will work in its usual way, but it will open and close when the input signal reaches the set threshold, rather than the audio from the channel it is inserted on. As with a sidechain-activated compressor, the plug-in will work completely independently.

You can use any rhythmical element in your production (or even one that isn't) to trigger your gate – you can even program a percussion groove specifically to trigger your gate. Some really energetic sequences can be

Power Tip
You may have found, when you're using a kick drum or other percussion part to trigger your sidechain, that the effect drops out in certain parts of your tracks. This is, of course, simply because that particular percussion part is not actually playing. To remedy this situation you can use what's called a 'ghost part'. This, as the name suggests, is a duplicate of the trigger audio without any gaps or breaks, routed to no output, so it isn't heard.

constructed this way and, considering the fact that you can fine-tune the attack, release and threshold settings of your gate, the freedom here is really quite impressive.

Special FX and modulators

There are some plug-ins within Logic Pro that you may not expect to accept sidechain signal at all, but they do. Processors such as the AutoFilter, RingShifter and EVOC 20 TrackOscillator can all be used with a sidechain input, enabling you to take these already creative processors one step further.

Try running a vocal line through the RingShifter using a drum loop as your sidechain for some freaky rhythmical effects – there are even presets to accommodate this sort of process. The AutoFilter can produce equally impressive sounds and will enable you to create custom envelopes to automate your filter movements. **MTF**

STEP-BY-STEP Using a noise gate to create rhythmical patterns.

1 Choose the sound you want to treat with the gate effect. Sustained sounds such as strings, pads and leads work well here but feel free to experiment with FX samples and vocals as well. Create a loop around the sound so it plays continuously. This will be useful later.

2 Insert one of Logic Pro's gate plug-ins into this new sound; either the Silver Gate or the more complex Noise Gate can accept sidechain inputs. I have chosen the simpler Silver Gate for this example, just to keep things clear.

3 Initialise the gate by zeroing all the parameters. You should now hear no sound on your treated channel. If you are not sure how to initialise a gate, simply copy these settings. Logic's Noise Gate can use similar settings, as can any third-party plug-in.

4 Locate the sound you want to trigger your gate effect; percussive sounds will fare best. Try using well-defined loops or samples – or even program your own using Ultrabeat or the EXS24. If you don't want to hear this sound, route it to No Output.

5 In the gate plug-in, select the new percussion channel in the Side Chain dropdown menu. You still won't be able to hear any sound at this point, due to the gate control's being initialised, but the sidechain is now set up and the audio should be flowing correctly.

6 Don't bring the gate threshold down until you hear the peaks of the percussion triggering the process and enabling audio to pass. Once you are happy with the threshold you can adjust the attack and release settings. You should now hear a rhythmical gate pattern.

LOGIC PRO 8 WORKSHOP

ON YOUR **MusicTech DVD** Full-sized screenshots and all the supporting files you'll need to follow this tutorial.

MAINSTAGE

MainStage offers an exciting new twist on performing live with Logic Pro's instruments and effects. **Mark Cousins** treads the boards.

For performing keyboard players, Logic Pro has always been regarded as one of the most fully featured packages available, mainly thanks to its range of vintage instruments, which includes Rhodes, Hammond and clavinet emulations. As good as these sound sources are, however, all DAWs present a couple of major stumbling blocks when it comes to live performance. Firstly, there are the cramped GUIs – fine for studio use, but almost unreadable on a dark stage. Then you need to organise your patches. Do you have one song for a whole set with each sound on a different track, or load different settings for each piece? Finally, there's the process of getting your control hardware to map to your software instruments, a skill that seems to necessitate several hours hunched over a MIDI specification chart.

If you've ever tried to use virtual instruments live, MainStage will stick out as one of the most exciting new additions in the Logic Studio package. Put simply, there's

WITH FORETHOUGHT, YOU CAN ASSEMBLE A SYSTEM THAT SPECIFICALLY RELATES TO YOUR CONTROL HARDWARE.

no other system that offers such an effective solution for using plug-in instrument technology live. With a little bit of planning and forethought, you can assemble a system that specifically relates to your control hardware, maps and organises all your patches, provides hands-on control over a range of instruments and plug-ins, and is presented clearly enough to be seen a few metres or more away from your computer.

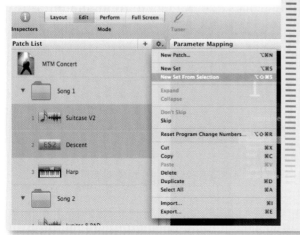

Power Tip

Hidden in the Actions folder are a number of AppleScripts that can be used to remotely control iTunes. Configured with Concert-level buttons, the AppleScript actions offer you a great way of controlling your backing tracks with a MIDI keyboard. Simply set up a suitable playlist in iTunes and have MainStage locate, play and move through each song using the Next Track, Previous Track and Play/Pause AppleScripts.

Power Tip

One of the most useful features in MainStage is its ability to organise and juggle the running order of your performance. Patches can be organised into sets, which seem to make the most sense when used to differentiate between the various songs in your performance. The feature is similar to the Play List concept in iTunes – you simply highlight the required patches and then select New Set From Selection from the Patch List menu. You can reorganise both the order of the set folders and, of course, the order of the patches within them.

Key concepts

We'll start exploring MainStage by looking at some of the pre-assembled concert templates included with the application. A Concert file contains all of MainStage's settings and parameters, from the on-screen layout of controls to the mapping of plug-in parameters and, most importantly, the organisational data for the patches being used. Try loading the Assortment template from the Keyboard Collection and exploring its contents in Edit mode (the four modes are toggled from the top left corner); just browse through the various patches. **1**

Although you can edit these pre-designed templates, it makes more sense to build your own. This enables you to design a layout that matches your MIDI controllers, and to assemble sounds that relate specifically to the songs in your set. To create an initialised concert, choose New Concert from the File menu, go to the Others Collection and select Starter Concert. **2**

Layout

In MainStage's Layout mode you can design a virtual representation of your MIDI hardware alongside any additional screen-based controls. To begin creating your virtual rig, drag and drop objects from the Panel Controls palette and the Shelf Controls palette at the bottom of the screen. Alongside the obvious elements – a keyboard, modulation wheel and so on – you can also insert a collection of knobs and/or sliders, level meters, drum pads and even image files. If you need to, you can also cut and paste objects from other Concerts. **3**

Once you've designed some on-screen controls, you'll need to map them to your physical MIDI controls. If you've got the Layout Inspector open on the left side of the screen, you should be able to activate the Learn button and wiggle the accompanying MIDI controller. The on-screen controller will map to it. **4**

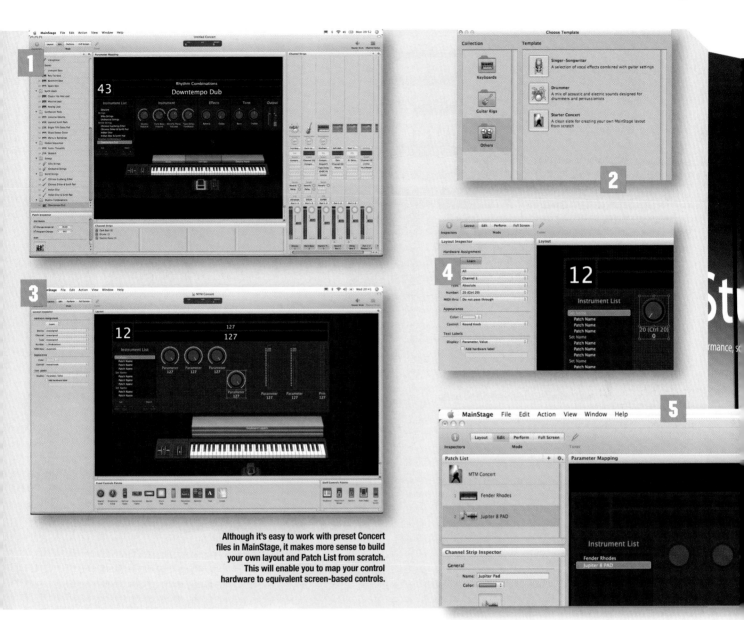

Although it's easy to work with preset Concert files in MainStage, it makes more sense to build your own layout and Patch List from scratch. This will enable you to map your control hardware to equivalent screen-based controls.

With the layout designed and mapped, you need to create your patches in Edit mode. The Patch List is viewable on the left side of the interface, with a default patch assigned to a Fender Rhodes sound on the EVP88. Let's leave this default patch for now and create a new patch, using the plus sign in the top right corner of the Patch List. Again, you'll find the EVP88 as a default assignment, so select the Reset Channel Strip from the Channel Strip Settings box at the bottom of the interface to create a fresh starting point.

Each instance of a patch can be assigned its own parameters, instruments and effects, so create an instance of your chosen virtual instrument followed by any EQ, compression or effects you feel appropriate. We've chosen an instance of Arturia's Jupiter-8V – just to prove that MainStage works with third-party instruments and effects! – plus a small amount of sweetening EQ. We've also named the patch in the Patch list as well as the channel strip using the Channel Strip Inspector. **5**

In control

Now the exciting bit. Remember the controls we created in Layout mode, which now appear greyed-out and inactive? Well, by clicking on any one of the unassigned

ports and pressing the Map Parameters button in the Screen Control Inspector, you can map the plug-in's controls to the relevant on-screen control. As these are already mapped to external MIDI controls, you can now manipulate key parameters physically and, with different settings for each patch, you can custom-design each mapping to reflect the needs of the patch in question. **6**

Taking the concept a stage further, you can also use MainStage to create custom stacks, or 'splits', of virtual instruments for each patch. To add a new instrument, go to the Channel Strips section and click on the small plus symbol. In this example we've created a straight layer of Jupiter-8V and some strings from the EXS24, but you can click on an individual channel strip and set different Key Ranges using the Channel Strip Inspector. **7**

Concert-Level mapping

Another important MainStage concept to grasp is the difference between Patch-Level mapping and Concert-Level mapping. So far, we've only dealt with Patch-Level mapping – in other words, controls that specifically relate to the sound in question. However, it's also possible to set global performance-level assignments for controls that remain the same irrespective of the patch being used.

Power Tip

Split points – like those found on many controller keyboards – generally tend to be at fixed points along the range of a keyboard. In the case of MainStage, though, you can define a so-called 'floating split', which dynamically changes the split point according to where you are on the keyboard and what instruments are being triggered. Increase the floating split at either end of a channel strip's Key Range to create the range you require.

MainStage provides the perfect bridge between your hardware's MIDI controls and the various parameters of an instrument or effects plug-in. The specific mapping to your chosen plug-in controls can vary between patches, enabling you to precisely match its settings to your on-stage requirements.

LIVE PERFORMANCE WITH VIRTUAL INSTRUMENTS HAS BECOME SIGNIFICANTLY EASIER TO ACHIEVE THANKS TO MAINSTAGE.

▶ To access Concert-Level assignments, you'll need to click on the corresponding Concert icon in the Patch list. By clicking on an object you can set various parameter mappings – such as the master volume or the level metering of outputs 1/2 – that can be accessed by every patch. What's particularly interesting, though, are the options contained in the Actions folder, which include the ability to navigate between patches, display current patch names and so on. 8

Another important area that relates to Concert-Level editing is global effects – reverb and delay, for example – being sent from the instrument. Try creating a buss send from one or more instruments in a given patch. You should notice an accompanying buss master fader being created, though if you move back to the Concert icon at the top of the Patch List you'll see that the new buss is now part of the Concert-Level assignments. This enables any patch to access these effects, as well as offering the ability to create a single object to control aspects like the reverb level. 9

Power Tip

To move sounds between existing Logic projects and your MainStage Concert file, use the Channel Strip Settings features. You'll need to save your instrument channel in Logic as well as any buss-based effects you've used. Consider creating folders as you save the patches, to enable you to identify sounds and songs. The Channel Strip settings can be recalled in MainStage when you create a new patch or channel strip in Edit mode.

Going live

With your patch assigned and mapped, you're ready to perform your MainStage Concert. Moving to Performance mode enables you to see and interact with a large-scale layout, with the Full Screen option devoting the whole of your screen real estate to MainStage. What's more, although we've illustrated the MainStage concept working on the assumption of a gigging keyboard player, there's no reason why you can't adapt this technology for any 'instrumental' performer using plug-in technology – whether it's a guitarist playing through Guitar Amp Pro or a drummer using trigger pads and drum loops. If you need any further inspiration, check out some of the other example concert templates included with MainStage. 10

It seems somewhat surprising that one of the most cutting-edge developments in the Logic Studio package lies away from the Logic Pro application itself, but in creating MainStage, Apple really seems to have hit the mark in respect to creating an inspiring and flexible tool to solve a specific musical problem. Without doubt, live performance with virtual instruments has become significantly easier to achieve thanks to MainStage, and, most importantly, it can be done in a way that suits the development of a live set, whether that's in a noisy practice room or the crowded, dark and sweaty environment of the stage. MTF

LOGIC PRO 7 WORKSHOP

MULTI-INSTRUMENTS

Have you ever been confused about the best way to integrate multi-instruments like Logic's EXS24 into your projects? **Mark Cousins** goes through the options.

Multi-instruments have played an important role in music production for some time now, whether in the form of multi-timbral workstations like Roland's JV-2080 or in the form of more in-depth virtual instruments like Kontakt 2 or BFD. But when it comes to integrating these monsters into your Logic Pro session, it's not always clear what the best approach is. Do you, for example, run multiple instances of instruments like Kontakt? Or is it easier to access their extra channels by adjusting the MIDI output from your controller keyboard? And then there's the tricky matter of multiple outputs. Do they appear automatically? Or will you have to modify the Environment to access them?

Virtual instruments tend to fall into two groups: those that generate a single sound assigned to one MIDI channel, and those that use a number of MIDI channels, each with a different patch assigned to it. Good examples of these alternative approaches in action are Logic Pro's EXS24 and Native Instruments' Kontakt. The EXS24 interface is designed to have only one patch loaded into it at any time – if you want multiple sounds running

Power Tip

Logic's EXS24 comes in a multi-channel version, so you can route individual zones and/or grouped zones to additional outputs. If you're using the EXS24 as a drum sampler, you can apply different reverb, compression and EQ settings to each part of the kit. An alternative application would be to use the multi-channel functionality for 5.1 surround sound production, where each zone, or group, could send samples to specific surround channels.

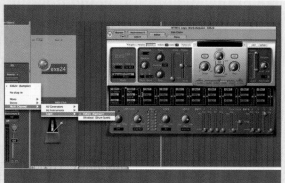

YOU CAN RECORD, MOVE AND DISTRIBUTE PARTS WITHOUT HAVING TO WORRY ABOUT RE-ASSIGNING CHANNEL DATA.

simultaneously, you have to run multiple instances. Kontakt, on the other hand, presents up to 16 concurrent MIDI channels, with any number of patches assigned to them. The assumption is that you will make full use of those MIDI channels, running multiple instances only when you run out of MIDI channels. **1**

One of the biggest hurdles when you're running virtual instruments with more than one MIDI channel is the lack of an intuitive way of accessing these extra channels. By default, Logic assigns each of its virtual instruments to MIDI channel 1, as indicated in the Instrument Parameters dialogue. By changing the setting to All you should at least be able to access all the channels from a MIDI keyboard transmitting on the appropriate setting. **2**

The MIDI solution

A much more elegant solution to setting up your MIDI keyboard is to make some modifications to Logic's Environment window and augment the MIDI routing of the virtual instruments in question. To do this, first open the Environment window and go to the Audio layer. Locate

the instance of the instrument you want to have full MIDI access to and select New>Multi Instrument. Logic will now create a new multi-instrument that you can name as you see fit and position just below the instrument's fader. While you're at it, uncheck the 16 MIDI channels so that they all become accessible. **3**

To make the new multi-instrument work you'll need to physically connect it to the virtual instrument's fader. To do this, click and hold on the small arrow and drag it up to the fader. If you've done this correctly, Logic will ask you if you want to remove the current port assignments. Click Yes and a short virtual patchlead should connect the two objects. **4**

Making arrangements

To access the virtual instrument you'll need to drag the newly created multi-instrument to a spare track in the Arrange window. You should now have 16 tracks, representing the 16 MIDI channels of the virtual instrument. Simply by resting on any one of the tracks, the MIDI data will be routed to the appropriate channel destination on the virtual instrument. What's more, you can record, move and distribute parts without having to worry about re-assigning channel data. **5**

Another type of multi-instrument is one that features multiple audio outputs. Good examples are drum-based samplers like FXpansion's BFD or XLN Audio's Addictive Drums. Multiple audio outputs are vital for these types of applications because the ability to send individual kit mics to discrete channels in Logic's mixer is highly desirable. Start setting up your multiple outputs by initiating the multi-channel version of the plug-in, which should be accessible from just below the main Stereo branch of your Plug-ins folder. **6**

To access the additional outputs from your virtual instrument, you'll need to incorporate the Aux Input

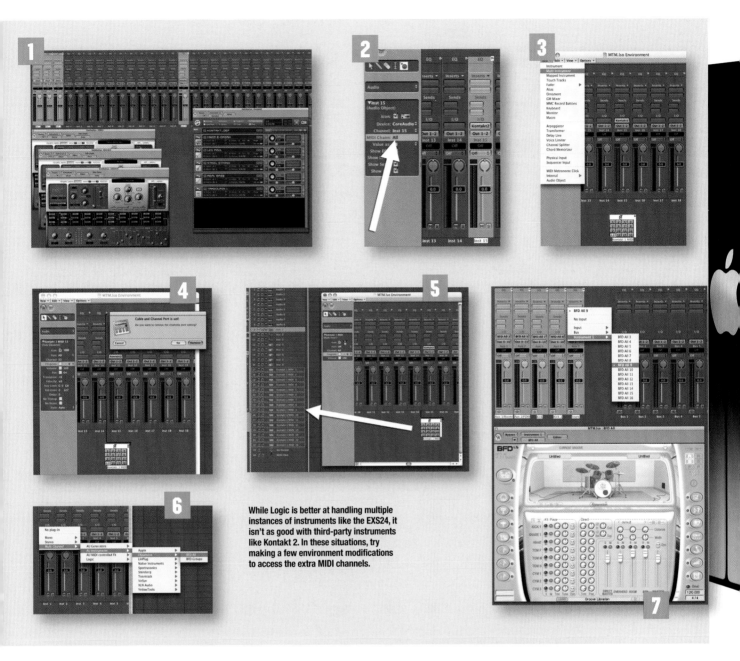

While Logic is better at handling multiple instances of instruments like the EXS24, it isn't as good with third-party instruments like Kontakt 2. In these situations, try making a few environment modifications to access the extra MIDI channels.

object into the audio environment. As the name suggests, an aux input's usual role is to route external signals into a mix –such as a feed coming from an external mixer, for example – but you can also use aux inputs to access a multi-channel instrument's additional outputs. To do this, find a spare aux input and click on the Input Selection tab (just above the Output tab). In the pop-out list you should see the usual Input and Bus options, but you should also see new options for the instruments you've created with multiple outputs. **7**

It takes time to set up all 16 outputs, and you'll have to create additional aux input objects – to do this, simply cut and paste the existing objects and change their channel status accordingly – but once this is done you'll be able to apply individual effects, EQ and compression to each output as you desire. Coupled with the techniques outlined above for dealing with multiple MIDI channels, you could almost get back to the 'ideal' of having multiple instances – though, of course, you're saving a significant amount of DSP resources by running a single instance rather than 16.

Logic Pro's system for handling multi-instruments isn't the smoothest, most intuitive solution you can find, but it does provide immense functionality, as well as the ability to integrate multi-channel/output instruments as you see fit. And there are many more labour-saving techniques to exploit in Logic, such as creating song templates for typical setups, and/or copying and pasting environment objects between songs. Employing these techniques will make the technical processes behind creating music considerably smoother. **MTF**

Power Tip

When you drag a multi-instrument from the Environment window to the Arrange window, you can create new tracks in two ways. To transfer all 16 MIDI channels, make sure none of the channels are selected on the multi-instrument or only the corresponding MIDI channel will transfer. This feature prevents your arrangement being swamped by 16 MIDI channels when you only actually need one.

Logic Pro controllers

While you can control Logic with just your keyboard and mouse, a few dedicated controllers will make life considerably easier. **Mike Hillier** selects his favourites.

The computer keyboard and mouse are remarkable pieces of equipment, enabling you to access a huge number of different functions and perform a wide range of tasks, but they are generalised tools and for editing and mixing music inside Logic they are far from the most intuitive ways of getting things done.

When it comes to mixing, having simultaneous access to several knobs and faders can enable you to construct your mixes much faster, riding faders more accurately and – unlike with a mouse – you can control more than one parameter at the same time.

The control surfaces available today range from basic MIDI-based models, which usually need to be carefully configured to control various aspects of Logic, to dedicated high-end controllers with flying faders and built-in integration with your host.

Here are some of the best.

BUDGET MODELS UP TO £150
Entry-level devices that do the job well enough.

Frontier Design AlphaTrack

Manufacturer **Frontier Design Group** Price **£150**

Contact **Sonic8 08701 657456**

Web **www.frontierdesign.com**

→ "One fader to rule them all" is the phrase used to sum up AlphaTrack on Frontier Design's website. It's a very apt description because, if you think about it, mix automation is often carried out on a track-by-track basis. That's the design rationale behind the AlphaTrack, which also features transport buttons, touch-sensitive encoders, a 32-character backlit display and a unique touch-sensitive jog/shuttle strip. The fader and three encoders are a real boon to mixing, providing quick control over levels, pans, sends, EQs, plug-ins and automation. It surely can't be long before most project studios are equipped with AlphaTrack or something similar.

VERDICT ★★★★★★★★★☆☆

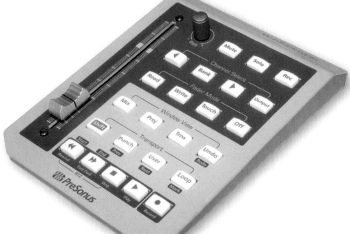

PreSonus FaderPort

Manufacturer **PreSonus** Price **£119**

Contact **Source Distribution 020 8962 5080**

Web **www.presonus.co.uk**

← The FaderPort is a sturdy piece of kit in an all-metal case that fits neatly on a desktop without hogging too much space. Getting around Logic with the FaderPort was surprisingly quick and simple. Three buttons provide instant access to the main recording windows: Project, Mixing and Transport. Selecting and arming tracks is just as easy. Adjacent tracks are selected with left and right buttons or by holding down a special Bank button to skip eight tracks at once.

VERDICT ★★★★★★★★☆☆

MID-RANGE MODELS £150 – £230
More buttons: more functionality: more control.

Novation ReMOTE Zero SL

Manufacturer **Novation** Price **£229**

Contact **Novation 01494 462246**

Web **www.novationmusic.com**

Novation turned the USB MIDI controller market upside down when it released the ReMOTE SL series, which again showed the company's knack for making ground-breaking studio gear. These were the first controllers to incorporate Novation's revolutionary AutoMap software. The SL Zero does away with the keyboard, instead providing you with a bank of MIDI controls that can be used to control Logic alongside any conventional MIDI keyboard. Now in its second revision, the AutoMap software is even more impressive, taking control of nearly everything in Logic with minimal user interaction.

VERDICT ★★★★★★★★★☆

Tascam FireOne

Manufacturer **Tascam** Price **£210**

Contact **TEAC UK 0845 130 2511**

Web **www.tascam.com**

The FireOne by Tascam and the Frontier Design Group marries a two-in, two-out FireWire audio interface with basic DAW controls, including a jogwheel, transport controls and function keys for controlling a variety of basic DAW functions. While standard mixing features like faders, pan pots and solo/mute switches will always be far more useful than a jogwheel and function keys, you could always combine the FireOne with Frontier Design's AlphaTrack for a more complete hands-on experience.

VERDICT ★★★★★★★★★☆☆

M-Audio UC-33e

Manufacturer **M-Audio** Price **£190**

Contact **M-Audio 01923 204010**

Web **www.maudio.co.uk**

The UC-33e is a flexible and highly useful MIDI controller that will find a place in most setups. The unit is laid out like an eight-channel mixer, each channel having a fader and three rotary encoders. There's also a master volume fader, plus 14 assignable buttons and a set of programming buttons. Among the useful features on the UC-33e is a snapshot feature, which sends the entire settings to Logic so you can store and recall mixer and effect settings.

VERDICT ★★★★★★★★★☆☆

AKAI MPD32

Manufacturer **Akai** Price **£220**

Contact **Numark Alesis 01252 341400**

Web **www.akaipro.com**

The more advanced music software becomes, the greater people's desire for more hands-on control over it. The MPD32 combines MPC pad-style composition and beat-making tools with a more conventional MIDI control surface to take some of the pain out of setting up software control. It fulfils both of these roles well, being fun to play, yet capable as a control surface. Whether you're a beat-maker or you just want more hands-on control over your software, the MPD32 is a strong contender.

VERDICT ★★★★★★★★★☆

HIGH-END MODELS UP TO £1,000
For the serious studio engineer.

FATAR NUMA

Manufacturer **Fatar** Price **£900**

Contact **Arbiter 020 8207 7880**

Web **www.fatar.com**

→ Fatar's Studiologic line of keyboards has traditionally focused on the concept of MIDI control and quality keyboard action rather than anything particularly fancy, and so it remains with their latest offering. The real appeal of the Numa, like so many of Fatar's products, is its playability, though a nagging doubt persists over its price, considering the limited feature set. This is a very playable master keyboard, but it does seem a little short on features.

VERDICT ★★★★★★★☆☆☆

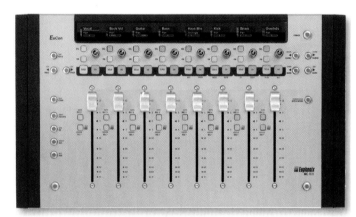

Euphonix MC Mix

Manufacturer **Euphonix** Price **£699**

Contact **Euphonix**

Web **www.euphonix.com/artist**

← The MC Mix is one of two new Euphonix Artist Series products aimed at the project studio owner. It provides eight 100mm touch-sensitive motorised faders, along with eight rotary controls. Unlike similar systems, which use MIDI or USB connectivity, the MC Mix connects over Ethernet using proprietary EuCon software. This can support up to four MC Mix or (its sibling) MC Master controllers. We see the MC Mix as the first step in the next generation of control surfaces. It is hard to think of a more feature-packed, elegant solution for DAW-based mixing.

VERDICT ★★★★★★★★★☆

Mackie Control Universal Pro

Manufacturer **Mackie** Price **Originally £999**

Contact **Loud Technologies 01268 571212**

Web **www.mackie.com**

→ Striking one of the best balances between cost and performance, Mackie's Control Universal Pro provides almost seamless integration with Logic alongside nine Penny+Giles touch-sensitive faders, rotary encoders, channel strip, function and transport controls. Despite its 'Pro' tag, hugely improved build quality and additional functionality, Mackie has kept an eye on price. A full system isn't cheap, but as the front end to Logic, no other controller provides this level of elegance and integration. And when it comes to controlling your DAW, is it really worth compromising?

VERDICT ★★★★★★★★★☆

TOP OF THE RANGE – £10,000+
Crikey, you could buy a farmhouse in France for that.

SSL Matrix

Manufacturer **SSL** Price **£14,687**

Contact **Sound Technology 01462 480000**

Web **www.solid-state-logic.com**

→ The Matrix combines the best of the analogue and digital worlds, and integrates your DAW with any outboard processors and mic pre-amps you may have. Each of the 16 channels on the desk can be used as analogue inputs, or as motorised, touch-sensitive DAW controllers. The Matrix also has 16-DAW returns, enabling you to mix stems from your DAW in the analogue signal path of the Matrix.

VERDICT ★★★★★★★★★☆

It's a feel thing

NUMA

Elegance, innovation and personalisation combine to create NUMA - the first professional keyboard controller to realise that not everyone plays the same way.

Photographed at KMR Audio, London. T: 020 8445 2446. www.kmraudio.com

Grand Hammer Action

The new Studiologic Grand Touch keyboard features our most sophisticated graded touch action yet. Increased throw-distance simulates a full concert grand piano.

Easy Control System

Using new touch-sensitive technology, the user-interface allows clear, efficient and intuitive programming.

Intelligent Dynamics

The most advanced custom velocity response system ever developed guides you quickly and easily to your personal optimum dynamic touch.

Innovative Design

Slide the aluminium cover to increase surface area for your laptop or other control surface. Also includes removable transparent music stand.

STUDIOLOGIC®

www.arbiter.co.uk

GET FUNKY WITH THE EVD6

Logic Pro's EVD6 faithfully re-creates the sound of the Hohner Clavinet, but how do you use it to produce a suitably vintage performance? **Mark Cousins** gets funky.

Thanks to Stevie Wonder's infectiously rhythmic playing on *Superstition*, the clavinet – which is basically a clavichord with pickups – has become one of the funkiest instruments ever built. Following on from the authenticity and detail of Logic Pro's other vintage instruments, the EVD6 keeps the spirit of the clavinet very much alive and well, retaining all the clavinet's controls and a host of essential effects – including distortion, compression, phasing and wah – that have become integral to the sound we all know and love. But for newcomers to the clavinet – or indeed the EVD6 – how do you combine these elements to create an effective and suitably 'funkalicious' performance?

Beneath the bonnet, the EVD6 bears a strong resemblance to Logic Pro's principal physical modelling synthesizer, Sculpture. In effect, the EVD6 is another string-based component modelling synth, demonstrating a precise understanding of the clavinet's response to its strings being struck and how this is conveyed via the attached pickups. In short, what this means is that the EVD6 offers both a surprisingly accurate and expressive

FEW CLAVINET PERFORMANCES IN THE 70S WOULD HAVE BEEN COMPLETE WITHOUT THE ADDITION OF AN EFFECT.

re-creation of the clavinet sound, but (and this is where its slightly complex interface can put people off) the EVD6 can also be pushed far beyond the physical and acoustic limits of the original instrument.

Rocker switches

Copy the file Tutorial.lso from the *MTF* DVD to your hard drive and open it. First, try experimenting with the original clavinet rocker switches, which control the filter and pickup selection. The filter is a little strange, with each rocker switch changing the raw sound in a unique way, while also offering the possibility of combining the various settings to create hybrids. For example, selecting the Brilliant switch provides the brightest clavinet tone – great for cutting through a mix – whereas the Soft position makes the tone more muted. Combining the switches – Brilliant, Treble, Medium and Soft – produces the fullest tone, whereas combining spaced tones – Treble with Soft, for example – can be a great way of producing a more hollow timbre. ▣

Another way of varying the tone is to experiment with

Power Tip

For a more varied set of production objectives, try bypassing either Guitar Amp Pro's Amplifier or Speaker models. For example, using the DI Box Speaker setting removes speaker colouration, leaving just the distorted output. This produces a brighter, brasher distortion with more high harmonics than that produced via the speaker. You could also use Clean Tube Amp (again, sans speaker) to provide gentle preamp-like distortion for vocals.

guitar amp pro

the pickup selection, which works in much the same way as on an electric guitar. Various combinations of the rocker switches (C/D and A/B) will deliver different shades of warmth or nasality, which can all help your clavinet to sit appropriately in the mix.

Moving beyond the original restrictions of the instrument, though, Logic's EVD6 also enables you to transform the pickup's output into a stereo signal (the original device had only a mono output) using the Stereo Spread control. Going further still, you can even move the physical positions of the pickups themselves, altering both the width and the timbre of the sound. ▣

Modifying the String parameters – in the top left corner of the interface – gets you into the real nitty-gritty of string modelling, though some of these are more musically effective than others. Try experimenting with the damping controls – as featured on the original clavinet's damping slider and pre-assigned to the mod wheel – alongside the Click Intensity to cut or boost the clavinet's distinctive key-click sound. ▣

Few clavinet performances in the 70s would have been complete without the addition of an effect, and in this respect the EVD6 gives you plenty to play with. Some basic effects to check out include the phaser, which creates a fantastically swirly 70s vibe, and distortion. Increasing the intensity of the modulation section effects, which also include a flanger and chorus as well as the aforementioned phaser, increases the level of the phaser in the EVD6's output. With distortion, you could either use the EVD6's internal distortion section or Guitar Amp Pro to emulate recording the original instrument through a Fender Twin amplifier. ▣

The Wah section enables you to dynamically modulate the sound of the clavinet, either manually, using an assignable MIDI controller – the default is CC 04 Footpedal – or automatically, in response to the envelope

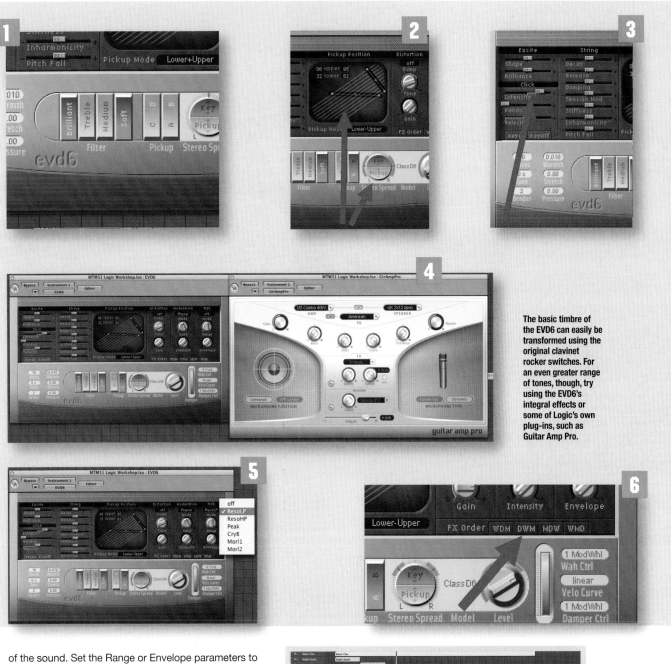

The basic timbre of the EVD6 can easily be transformed using the original clavinet rocker switches. For an even greater range of tones, though, try using the EVD6's integral effects or some of Logic's own plug-ins, such as Guitar Amp Pro.

of the sound. Set the Range or Envelope parameters to specify the amount of modulation depth you want to apply via MIDI or the auto-wah section respectively. The different modes – ResoLP, ResoHP, Peak, CryB, Morl1 and Morl2 – differentiate between various designs of wah-wah pedal. The ResoLP, for example, can be a great way of darkening the EVD6's output – something that is especially effective in more exposed passages – while the CryB, Morl1 and Morl2 create the more familiar nasal sound of wah-wah.

Chaining

As with all effects, the order in which they are chained together can have a big impact on the results, especially if both wah and distortion come into play. Usefully, though, the EVD6 enables you to switch the order of its effects via the small tab – try using the Cry Baby setting and experimenting with the distortion before (DWM, for example) and after (WMD) the wah-wah.

As with all of Logic's vintage instruments, the EVD6 demands to be played and actively 'tweaked' by hand.

Even though its basic palette of sounds is slightly more limited than a full-blown subtractive synthesizer, it's amazing just how much sonic variation can be coaxed out of it by adjusting the filter settings, pickup positions and integral effects. Going further still and exploring some of the other models beyond the basic D6 (accessible from the Model paramete) reveals an even greater range of tones, from a surprisingly effective Pluck – which is great for wah-wah guitar parts with a touch of extra damping – to dulcimers and sitars. MTF

Power Tip

If you're using the wah-wah feature of the EVD6, you may find it beneficial to use some form of compression to control erratic peaks. Though the EVD6 does have its own compressor, Logic Pro's standard Compressor plug-in offers far more control. Try using a fast attack (20ms), a hard ratio (5:1 and above), and the Peak Sensing mode to grab any problematic transients before they overload the main outputs.

Parallel compression techniques

Parallel compression is one of the best techniques for adding some extra punch and depth to our sound. Mo Volans demonstrates how easy it is to execute in Logic Pro 8.

Whether you're mixing a drum buss, processing vocals or mastering a whole track, parallel compression techniques may be just the thing you're looking for to add extra volume and depth to your Logic projects. With a little time and effort parallel bussing can breathe a new lease of life into your productions.

Using compressors to increase the punch and presence of an instrument is quite common practice during mixing sessions. With the right ratio, attack and release settings applied, a sound can be massively enhanced and characteristics beyond simple dynamics control can be added. On individual sounds, using a compressor as an insert is totally acceptable, but when you're treating groups of sounds, or an entire track, an alternative approach is often needed.

A solution that will afford you much more control over the balance of dry and processed signals is parallel compression, a technique that has been in the collective consciousness of sound engineers for some time now. Engineers in New York studios famously used the method to pump up drum tracks during the 70s disco era. Though

Power Tip

For a quick version of parallel compression, try the new Mix feature in Logic Pro's Compressor. You can experiment with this method by using the Compressor as an insert and accessing the Mix function in the lower part of the dropdown extended control panel. You can audition dry and processed versions of your sound using this method but don't expect the same flexibility and sound as a dedicated parallel compression buss.

some argue that parallel compression was actually born in Chicago, the so-called 'NYC technique' lives on in today's productions the world over. Though parallel compression is most commonly used for drum groups, it's not limited to this task and you should feel free to experiment with other areas of your mix.

Wet and dry

When you use parallel compression techniques in Logic, not only will you gain extra control but you can push the Compressor's settings to much more extreme levels. This is possibly due to the way the wet and dry signals are mixed. The technique involves sending all your chosen tracks to two independent groups: the first acts as the dry channel; the second is your wet, or processed, group.

Though the first of the two groups is referred to as 'dry', this doesn't mean there can't be any processing taking place here; subtle compression and EQ can be used to keep things in line. You're really aiming to let things breathe at this point, so steer clear or any hard limiting or overbearing saturation effects. As long as the group's original characteristics and dynamics are preserved you are on the right track.

The second group is where the action really takes place. A compressor is strapped across the buss as an insert and quite aggressive settings can be dialled in,

WITH A LITTLE TIME AND EFFORT PARALLEL BUSSING CAN BREATHE A NEW LEASE OF LIFE INTO YOUR PRODUCTIONS.

creating what would technically be considered an 'over-processed' sound. Many engineers use a classic compressor for this job; devices like the Universal Audio 1176LN are very popular here. Of course, not everyone has access to these expensive hardware compressors, but Logic Pro 8's own Compressor now supplies vintage modelling as standard – try the Opto and FET models as a really good starting point.

Once these two groups are set up the dry and

LOGIC MAKES THE CREATION OF NEW GROUPS A BREEZE WITH ITS NEW DYNAMIC BUSS ALLOCATION FEATURE.

processed sounds can be mixed to taste. You will soon realise the advantages this setup has over a simple compressor insert: not only does it add extra drive and character to your group of sounds, it actually considerably increases the perceived volume. When you're auditioning your dry group without the new parallel channel you may start to wonder how you ever managed without the technique of parallel compression.

Logic makes the creation of new groups a breeze with its new dynamic buss allocation feature. This system creates busses or groups as soon as you route a send or output to a new auxiliary channel. This is really useful as they appear in the mixer immediately, which generally improves workflow and keeps things organised.

Mastering

When it comes to mastering, parallel compression might not be the first technique you think of, but in some situations it can be perfect. Just as the method adds perceived volume in a mixing environment, it can do the same for your masters.

When simple compression and limiting just isn't cutting it, a heavily compressed duplicate of your track on a parallel channel can pump things up considerably without destroying the original dynamics of the track. This tends to work well with more minimal productions, so be warned: go down this route with an already busy track and you could end up with senseless noise.

Remember that both the parallel tracks are going to be fed through a chain of mastering processors straight after mixing. With this in mind you may not want to apply the same aggressive settings that you would in a mixdown scenario. Over-processing at this stage could lead to unwanted distortion and loss of presence.

A trick here is to try filtering the low-end frequencies from the effected parallel channel. Turning this channel up will now result in boosting the volume and density of the high frequencies in your master and leave the rest of your

STEP-BY-STEP Creating a parallel drum buss.

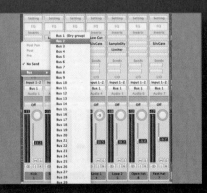

1 Construct your drum pattern using your usual method. It really doesn't matter if you are using audio or virtual instruments to generate your drum sounds, as long as each sound is on its own channel and can be routed to different outputs and busses.

2 Select all the sounds in your drum pattern in the Logic mixer. You can now route all the channels to a new buss with one movement. This first group will be your dry version of the drum signal and will represent an untreated, dynamic sound.

3 You can now apply any processing you may need on this first buss to keep things in line. In this example, not a huge amount was needed, so just a small amount of compression to iron things out was applied. Any EQ and filtering should be applied here.

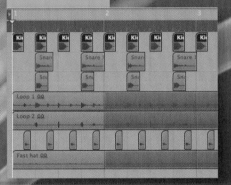

4 We'll now add the second, 'wet' group. Start by selecting all the tracks once again and routing their first send slot to a new group. As before, all tracks should conform in one easy operation. Once you're finished, check that all the send slots show the same information.

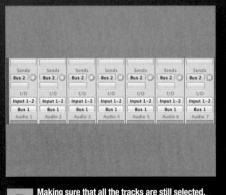

5 Making sure that all the tracks are still selected, turn the send levels up to around 0dB. This will ensure that a good amount of signal is sent to the wet group. You can always tweak this later if the setup is running too hot.

6 Now insert a compressor on the second buss and dial in some aggressive settings. A good tip here is to try the various component models included. You are now ready to mix the two signals together and hear the difference the process makes.

mix untouched. This can act as a form of dynamic exciter and give your master more 'air.'.

Compressors in series

An alternative approach to parallel processing is to use a number of compressors in series. This basically means using more than one insert on the same channel. Obviously, you lose the ability to fine-tune the balance of wet and dry signals and forgo the luxury of using extreme settings, but other benefits can sometimes make this method the weapon of choice.

If you are in a situation where you find that one compressor refuses to clamp down on rogue dynamics in a signal, try inserting another, similar compressor later in the chain, after any processors you may have in place. Surprisingly, two compressors with conservative settings in series can often have more impact than one compressor in overdrive. This technique of 'cascading' compressors in series can be one trick to try as an alternative to constructing a parallel buss. MTF

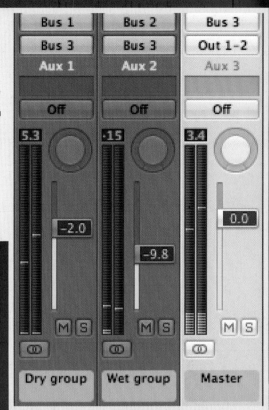

Power Tip

For added control when using parallel compression you can try adding a third master buss. Both your dry and effected groups should be fed into this master channel. This will give you ultimate control over the whole drum mix and will help you avoid having to constantly re-adjust the balance between the two main signals. Any further processing needed can also be added to this track, such as final EQ, reverb or filtering.

AN ALTERNATIVE APPROACH TO PARALLEL COMPRESSION IS TO USE A NUMBER OF COMPRESSORS IN SERIES.

STEP-BY-STEP Parallel compression in mastering.

1 Import your pre-master as you usually would onto a single stereo track. It is important that the material is untreated and has a decent amount of headroom. The track also needs to be in the same bit depth as your working project, so if it was recorded in 24-bit this file should be 24-bit.

2 Create a fresh stereo track and name it accordingly. This track will accommodate the more processed version of the track but at this point no plug-ins should be applied and the levels and other settings should be left initialised.

3 Copy an exact duplicate of the pre-master to your new track. It's really important to ensure that the two tracks are perfectly aligned here. Double-check your snap settings and play back the two tracks together. You will soon notice if they aren't in sync.

4 Insert a compressor onto the second pre-master channel and start to change the settings. You can get away with a pretty hefty amount of gain reduction here, anything up to and even beyond 15dB. Slow attack and release times should get a good result.

5 Strike a balance between the tracks by slowly raising the level of the processed version; this will enable you to gain perspective on the mix. Most of the signal should be made up by the original pre-master, with the processed track complementing the overall sound.

6 Add your usual mastering chain to the master output and adjust the input to accommodate the two tracks. Obviously, levels will be considerably higher due to two signals entering the processor chain, as opposed to one in a normal mastering scenario.

LOGIC PRO 8 WORKSHOP

▶ ON YOUR
MusicTech DVD-ROM
Full-sized screenshots
and all the supporting
files you'll need to
follow this tutorial.

AUDIO EDITING

Quick Swipe comping and Take folders have revolutionised sound editing in Logic, offering significant improvements to productivity. **Mark Cousins** gets his scissors out.

As great as Logic Pro 7 was as an audio production package, its editing features felt somewhat clumsy and inefficient, especially when it came to dealing with multiple takes. While basic tasks such as region resizing, crossfades and so on were adequately handled, the editing process got decidedly more complicated if you had a number of passes – or takes – of the same part. Usually, this entailed creating multiple tracks, each assigned to the same audio output. Compared to Pro Tools' elegant Playlist, audio editing in Logic required a fair degree of experience and patience.

Logic 8 is, of course, better equipped to deal with a whole range of tasks, but none of the improvements is as fundamentally important as the developments to its audio-editing capabilities. Quick Swipe comping and the Take Folder system have revolutionised the way audio is recorded and edited in Logic, making the production process easier to manage while seamlessly incorporating the new capabilities into the creative workflow. In this workshop, we're going to take a closer look at these new features, and assess how they've redefined recording and editing in Logic.

Recording

Logic 8's approach to dealing with multiple takes becomes immediately apparent as soon as you start making your first recordings. For single takes, nothing has

Power Tip

By default, Logic 8 places a 20ms crossfade at any given Quick Swipe edit point. If you want to preserve transient detail, therefore, avoid editing on the beat, instead placing your edit 20ms or so before the start of the note (this is good general editing practice anyway). Under the General tab of Logic Pro>Preferences>Audio, you can also change the default crossfade time as well as the crossfade curve.

changed, but in situations requiring you to overdub onto an existing region, or to record in Cycle mode, you'll notice that Logic handles audio regions in a different way. In the Logic of old, this method of recording would result in multiple regions being created on top of each other; in the case of Cycle mode, it created a number of regions spread across consecutive tracks. In Logic 8, however, multiple takes are organised into a Take folder, which simplifies the process immensely. **1**

Take folders

One of the great benefits of the Take Folder system is that you don't have to create multiple tracks to audition and flip between takes; you can now switch between different takes simply by clicking on the small arrow in the top right corner of the Take folder. A list in the accompanying Take Folder menu enables you to identify and select the appropriate take to audition, rather than having to mute and un-mute different regions to hear them individually. **2**

From the same menu you can also perform two important housekeeping tasks: Delete Take and Rename Take. Use the Delete Take option when you know that a part won't be used; this will unclutter your project and so make it easier to navigate. Use the Rename Take option to organise and catalogue any recorded material you think you might use, perhaps naming takes according to their quality – 'strong vocal', for example. Rename Take is useful because although it might be clear how you intend to use a take when you record it, your strategy might not be so apparent several weeks later. **3**

Composites

Being able to switch between takes has obvious advantages, but the real strength of the Take Folder system lies in its ability to create a comp – short for

Power Tip

Try using folders as a way of organising your mix. Group related instruments in the Arrange area by selecting them and then packing them into a folder (Region>Folder>Pack Folder). As well as tidying the parts in the Arrange area, you'll also notice a slim Folder channel in the mixer that's devoid of controls. Double-click on this and you'll open up a mixer specific to the channels/instruments in question, rather than the entirety of your mix.

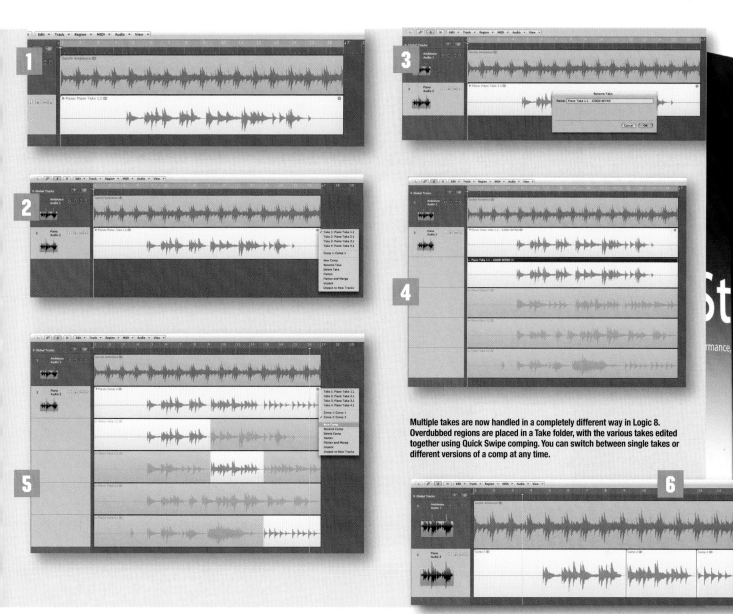

Multiple takes are now handled in a completely different way in Logic 8. Overdubbed regions are placed in a Take folder, with the various takes edited together using Quick Swipe comping. You can switch between single takes or different versions of a comp at any time.

composite – of several different recordings. As well as the various takes in the Take Folder menu, you should also see a list of comps – though at this stage you will only see the default comp created by Logic when you started recording. To view the comp, click on the small arrow in the top left corner of the Take folder. The folder should now explode to reveal the takes contained within it, as well as the current Quick Swipe edit points. **4**

Moving the Quick Swipe edit points between takes is as simple as dragging over the respective take to change the amount of highlighted audio. Notice how changes to one take are reflected in another (only one take can play at any time) and how the top line displays the current edit in its complete state, with hairlines indicating the edit point – these can be viewed even when the Take folder is closed. You can also create several different comps by selecting New Comp from the Take Folder menu. This will enable you to experiment with different treatments of the same material. **5**

One downside of the Quick Swipe Comping feature, though, is its inability to move a take from its recorded position in the Take folder – though, of course, you can move the position of the folder itself. This makes any minor timing refinements that you might have done

between multiple takes in Logic Pro 7 impossible to achieve with Logic 8's Take Folder system. However, as we'll see next, it is possible to revert to the old system for editing purposes.

Flattening

Finished – or even part-finished – comps can be handled in a number of ways. The first is to Flatten the edits you've made. Flattening has its advantages and disadvantages: on the one hand, you can't return to the edits in such an intuitive way as you can with the Quick Swipe Comping feature but, on the plus side, you will gain access to further ways of refining your edits that are impossible to achieve in Quick Swipe mode.

You can choose to flatten your edits via the Take Folder menu. The resulting output is displayed as a series of regions, with crossfades dividing them. Flattened in this way, you could choose to modify the timings of regions, for example, and/or the default crossfade times, using the same processes as you would when editing audio in Logic Pro 7. **6**

A more destructive version of the Flatten function is the Flatten and Merge option. Using Flatten and Merge will create a new file, complete with edit points and ▶

Power Tip

A feature that's easy to miss is the new Waveform Scaling option. Just like Pro Tools, the waveform can be expanded, effectively making the audio regions appear clipped – though they don't sound clipped – but at the same time, making it easier to visually edit quieter and more discreet elements of an audio file. To expand the waveform, click and hold on the Waveform icon next to the horizontal/vertical zoom controls and use the slider to scale accordingly.

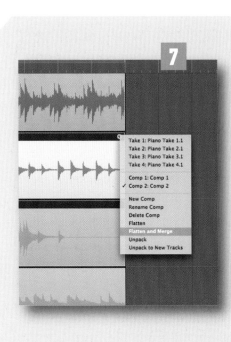

There are a number of ways of handling the comp when you've finished editing. Flattening will create a completed edit, with all the regions and crossfades in place. Unpacking the comp, however, might be more appropriate if you intend to carry out further work beyond the scope of the Quick Swipe Comping feature.

THE QUICK SWIPE COMPING AND TAKE FOLDER FEATURES BRING WITH THEM NEW LEVELS OF SPEED AND FLEXIBILITY.

▶ crossfades. If you're completely happy with your edits, Flatten and Merge could be an appropriate choice, especially if you want a more transportable version of the track to import into another DAW. Unless you specifically choose to delete the original takes, you'll always have the option of re-importing the files into the Arrange window should you want to revisit what you've done later on.

Unpacking
An alternative to flattening your edits is to Unpack the Take Folder. This places all your individual takes – along with the various comps, complete with crossfades – onto separate tracks. Unpacking the Take folder is messy in terms of the Arrange window and the number of tracks it can use up, but it does offer the best solution in terms of complete audio flexibility. For example, an unpacked take can easily be moved to new tracks – maybe using out-takes from a lead vocal as backing vocals. Or it might be that the remit of editing goes beyond what can be achieved with Quick Swipe comping alone – a vocal requiring pitch correction in Melodyne, for example, or elements of time compression and expansion.

The reverse of unpacking Take folders is to use the menu function Region>Folder>Pack Take Folder to combine several existing audio files into the same folder. The option to pack folders potentially solves any problems of addressing timing issues – simply Unpack the folder, move the required take and re-pack accordingly. This feature also offers an interesting way of creatively switching between a number of concurrent drum loops, packing them into a shared Take folder and then using Quick Swipe comping to create complicated jumps between the loops.

Major strength
If you've ever attempted any serious audio editing in Logic, you will have already realised that the Quick Swipe Comping and Take Folder features bring with them new levels of speed and flexibility. Working with multiple takes and the process of comping have been neatly redesigned to match the needs of today's studio and the production process as a whole. What was once a real weakness of the application has now become a major strength. It's also a very tangible reason to choose Logic Studio over the competition.

Whether you're patching together a rough vocal from a few vocal takes, or comping a full multi-track orchestral session, the process of audio editing in Logic has now become something to relish rather than something to avoid at all costs. MTF

Wireless In-Ear Monitor system,

a more compact option.

m3 system

m2 system

Tired of lugging heavy and cumbersome monitor equipment to each gig? Switch from traditional floor monitors to Audio-Technica's ultra-compact wireless-in-ear monitor systems for your live performances.

These rugged systems are built to stand up to the inevitable bumps of life on the road, delivering clear, natural sound for touring and installed-sound systems. Not only are they easy to transport, but they're also quick to set up.

Travel light on tour with Audio-Technica and focus on what really matters: your music.

Audio-Technica microphones are available from all good audio stores nationwide.

(A) audio-technica

always listening

LOGIC PRO 8 WORKSHOP

▶ ON YOUR
MusicTech DVD
Full-sized screenshots
and all the supporting
files you'll need to
follow this tutorial.

COMPRESSOR

Logic's Compressor is a valuable plug-in for all kinds of mixing tasks, especially now that several new features have been introduced. **Mark Cousins** makes some squash.

Compression is one of your important tools when it comes to the mixing process. It will restrain dynamic range to help a sound sit in place, and it is an effect in its own right. It's no surprise, therefore, that there are so many third-party compressors to choose from, each one dedicated to providing its own flavour of compression. But does this mean that Logic's own Compressor is somehow inferior in sound or performance?

Logic's integral Compressor is a tremendously versatile, workhorse plug-in, capable of producing everything from over-easy vintage compression to hard, transient-spanking drum squashing. This workshop takes a closer look at Logic's Compressor plug-in and explores the ways in which it can be applied within a Logic project. And, given the number of extra features that have been added to the Compressor in Logic 8 – including dedicated sidechain filtering, built-in limiting and various different circuit types – we'll also examine how these new and exciting features further what can be achieved with this already powerful and flexible plug-in.

Thresholds and ratios

Logic's Compressor is little different from most other compressors in that its two primary controls are Threshold (the point at which compression begins) and Ratio (the relative strength of compression), with the amount of 'squash' indicated by the gain reduction meter.

Even if you don't delve beyond these two basic parameters, you will still find lots of different approaches for the application of compression. Low Threshold and Ratio values (1.5:1-2:1), for example, will yield discreet dynamic control, with the compressor spending more

Power Tip

Another use for the Side Chain Filter is to turn the Compressor into a de-esser. With an instance of the Compressor placed across the vocal track, put the Side Chain Filter into Listen, change the mode to ParEQ and create a sharp boost in the region of the sibilance (around 4kHz). Change the Filter from Listen to On and adjust the Compressor so that it applies gain reduction whenever the sibilance occurs. This might require a ratio of about 6:1, with fast attack and release times.

time in compression, but with relatively small amounts of gain reduction (2-4dB, for example). A harder ratio (4:1 and above) will make the effect of compression more pronounced. Raising the threshold will cause the gain reduction to target louder points in the input – transients, for example. **1**

Having explored these two basic parameters, we can now begin to look at various refinements and softening treatments. One the most important controls for these types of task is the Compressor's Peak/RMS sensing. If that sounds complicated, think of the Peak/RMS switches as alternating the Compressor between a vintage-like response (RMS) and hard-acting digital compression (Peak).

Peak mode forces the Compressor to respond to the absolute signal level, which is great when you need precise amounts of gain control. RMS, on the other hand, responds to averaged signal levels – in much the same way as our ears do – to produce more musical, though slightly less responsive compression. **2**

Knees up

The knee of a compressor offers an additional means of producing a softer, more vintage-like compression effect. Many classic compressors – the Fairchild 670 or Teletronix LA-2A, for example – demonstrated a distinctly graduated move from no compression (a 1:1 ratio, for example) to the full ratio setting (3:1, for example). This results in a soft curve – also known as a knee – in the input/output graph on the compressor's control panel.

To help you visualise the knee, try setting a low Threshold (-19dB or so) and a hard Ratio (16:1) and then adjust the relative strength of the knee. To hear it, try adjusting the knee on the Compressor placed across the drum track in the Workshop file on the *MTF* DVD – soft knee settings produce a more 'rounded' compression; sharper knee settings direct the compressor more towards peak energy. **3**

Two incredibly important controls governing the movement and style of compression being applied are the Attack and Release parameters. In essence, attack and release govern the relative speed in and out of gain reduction. At fast attack settings the Compressor is quick to respond to movements above the threshold. A slow release, on the other hand, creates a lag between the input falling back below the threshold and the Compressor returning to its neutral state.

Although you'd initially expect an 'ideal' compressor to be fast and responsive, there are some distinct benefits to using softer settings. A slow attack, for example, will

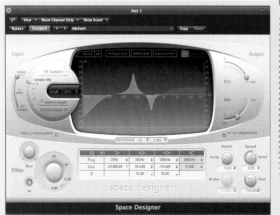

Power Tip

One significant improvement in Logic Pro 8 is the introduction of an equalizer as part of Space Designer. This is a particularly welcome addition, as equalization is often important in getting convolution reverb to sit correctly in the mix. For example, many of the natural impulse responses can sound slightly dark by comparison to other reverbs. Try a small amount of shelving boost at 12kHz and some bass rolloff below 100Hz to remedy this.

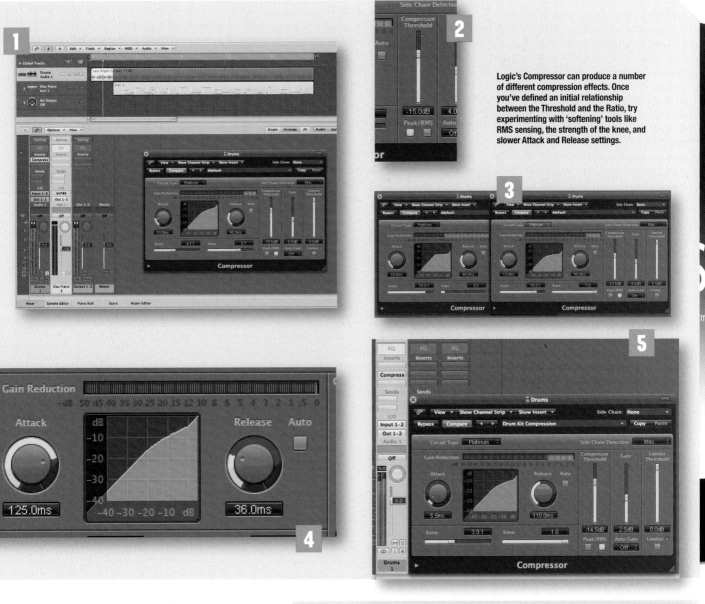

Logic's Compressor can produce a number of different compression effects. Once you've defined an initial relationship between the Threshold and the Ratio, try experimenting with 'softening' tools like RMS sensing, the strength of the knee, and slower Attack and Release settings.

preserve more of your input's transient energy, which is an important part of the life of a sound. Conversely, a slower release will sound less obtrusive, though some people actively enjoy the 'pumping' sound produced by faster release settings.

Gain control

Having looked at the style of compression, let's turn our attention to the output of the Compressor. As the process of applying gain reduction effectively reduces the amplitude of a signal, we need to restore the overall gain at the other end of the equation. Usefully, Logic provides an Auto Gain control that automatically compensates the output level based on the Threshold and Ratio settings, but it's often far better to manually restore the gain – using the Gain control – as the amount of Auto Gain applied is a few decibels more than is usually required. Ideally, you should aim to output identical peak levels for the uncompressed and compressed signals. This can be achieved by reference to the channels' meters.

Even with effective compression settings, you might still find that the occasional problematic transient slips through the net. The output limiter, therefore, provides a useful safety net in situations where the overall peak level

might be crucial. The only control is a single Threshold parameter, but at light settings the limiter can provide an extra layer of dynamic control, and prevent distortion further up the signal chain.

Circuit Type controls

Although Logic's Compressor has always been a useful tool to have to hand, there's no doubt that the new features introduced in Logic 8 significantly extend the usefulness of this convenient plug-in. One of the most noticeable changes has been the introduction of a

Power Tip

If you've loaded an Apple Loop file from your browser into Logic, it's likely that Logic will have instantiated a GarageBand instrument with a minimal control set. As an alternative, you can load the equivalent 'parent' instrument – such as the EXS24 sampler or ES2 synth – as indicated by the Instrument icon. Simply click on the current GarageBand instrument assignment and change it to the corresponding Logic instrument. All the settings will be transferred accordingly.

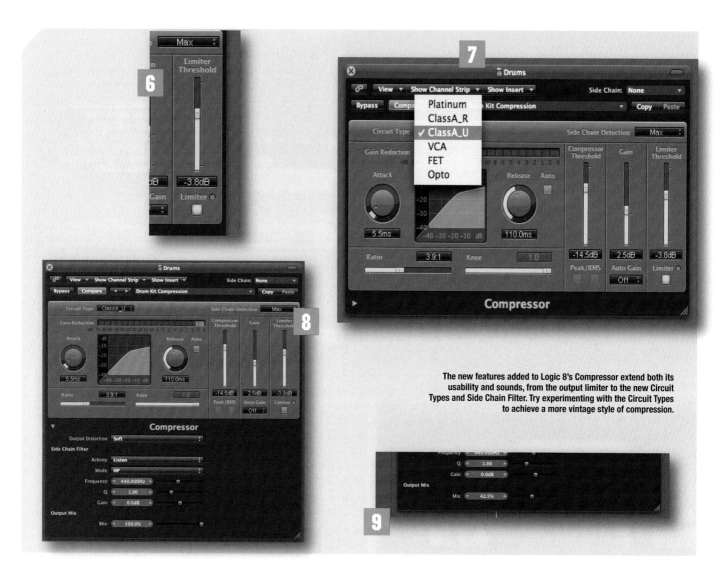

The new features added to Logic 8's Compressor extend both its usability and sounds, from the output limiter to the new Circuit Types and Side Chain Filter. Try experimenting with the Circuit Types to achieve a more vintage style of compression.

DESPITE STRONG COMPETITION FROM THIRD-PARTY PRODUCTS, LOGIC'S COMPRESSOR STILL HOLDS ITS OWN.

▶ selectable Circuit Type. Although the differences might appear to be subtle for first-time users, the Circuit Type controls seek to emulate some of the sound and performance characteristics of 'unspecified' classic compressors – though their names do provide some clues as to their origins.

Platinum is Logic's legacy setting (for compatibility with sessions created pre version 8); Classic A_R and Classic A_U possibly denote two Class A compressors; FET could be a Urei 1176; while Opto could be an LA-2A optical compressor. **7**

Switching between the different modes, even with the same panel settings, yields very different-sounding compression. This a palette worth exploring yourself, but you can achieve excellent results using the Class A_U on drums and vocals, while the softer control of the Opto mode works well on bass.

The exact nature of the modelling isn't explained, but it's interesting to note that the Peak/RMS modes and knee settings are both disabled on many of the circuit types, suggesting that these controls form a crucial part of the emulation taking place.

Power Tip

More than just another 'idiot button', the compressor's Auto Release control is an important tool for buss-based compression tasks. With a number of sounds being compressed at the same time, it can be hard to find a one-size-fits-all setting for the Release. The Auto switch, therefore, adapts the release time based on the programme material, finding the smoothest and most transparent-sounding settings for the compression taking place.

Side Chain Filter

From the Compressor's extended parameters it's now possible to access a unique Side Chain Filter as well as an Output Mix control. The Side Chain Filter enables you to change the frequency characteristics of what the compressors 'hears' and, hence, the type of compression achieved. For example, try using the HP (high-pass filter) setting across the drum loop, with a cutoff frequency of around 415Hz. Configured in this way, the compression should feel slightly airier than if the kick had been present in the sidechain input. You can also use the Listen mode in the Activity section to audition the filtering taking place, enabling you to establish optimum settings. **8**

The Mix control enables you to quickly set up an element of parallel compression – in other words, part of the uncompressed dry signal feeding back into the mix alongside the compressed version. Try using heavy, pumping compression – 6:1 ratio and up to 10dB of gain reduction – but roll back the mix to around 50% to bring back some of the transient energy. The result is a combination of the sound of 'compression' but without the original details being sucked out of the input. **9**

All squashed up

Despite strong competition from a variety of excellent third-party products, Logic's Compressor still holds its own. And if you haven't seen what the latest version can do, it's time to check it out. **MTF**

KRK SYSTEMS

Proudly distributed in the UK by

Focusrite®

SO PURE

NEW EXPOSÉ E8B AND VXT SERIES FROM KRK

Purity. Freedom from adulteration or contamination. That's what you need in the recording studio. Pure and simple uncoloured audio. KRK engineers understand this, and take great care to offer speakers that can be relied upon to deliver. The Exposé E8B and VXT series take studio monitoring to a whole new level. With an attention to detail and design expertise unmatched in the industry today KRK has truly raised the bar. Key design elements such as a sleek radiused edge enclosure with optimised airflow and minimal port turbulence, and finely tuned custom components, all ensure that the new Exposeé E8B and VXT series deliver a pure and realistic sound that is in a class of its own.

EXPOSÉ E8B   **VXT 6**   **VXT 8**   **VXT 4**

WWW.KRKSYS.COM

ACM

THE ACADEMY OF CONTEMPORARY MUSIC
WORLD LEADERS IN MUSIC INDUSTRY EDUCATION

get inspired
Full time courses in Music Production and Creative Sound Design.

get involved
"ACM is a place that brings together technology and musicians in a unique way. Music is after all, a collaborative art."
(Adrian Hall: Producer, Engineer, Mixer)

get heard
Unrivalled music industry connections.

THE ACADEMY OF CONTEMPORARY MUSIC
THE RODBORO BUILDINGS
BRIDGE STREET | GUILDFORD | SURREY GU1 4SB

THE QUEEN'S AWARDS
FOR ENTERPRISE:
INNOVATION
2008

Middlesex University

UNIVERSITY OF SURREY

Authorized Training Center
Education

enquiries@acm.ac.uk | www.acm.ac.uk | 01483 500 800

Logic Pro monitors

Studio monitors are the window into your mixes, so picking the right pair for your setup is a critical choice. Mike Hillier turns up the volume on some of the best.

To produce a good mix it is essential that you be able to hear an honest representation of that mix. Nearfield monitors have been designed specifically with this purpose in mind: to enable you to hear every part of your mix in a balanced and unflattering way. This philosophy runs counter to that of conventional hi-fi speakers, which aim to flatter your mix. Nearfield monitors enable you to see any flaws in your mix early on, so you can correct them.

Many engineers will have two or more pairs of nearfield monitors set up and will switch between them while mixing to see how their mix transfers to different equipment. Finding the right monitors is as much an art as mixing itself. Ask ten different engineers what their favourite monitors are and you are likely to get ten different answers, so test out several models before you invest. Take along a CD you know well and listen for the most neutral depiction of the sound.

MODERN CLASSICS
Monitors that grace many a studio.

Yamaha MSP7

Manufacturer **Yamaha** Price **£758**

Contact **Yamaha 01908 366700**

Web **www.yamaha-music.co.uk**

➡ Designed by Akira Nakamura, the father of the NS10, this is the cutting edge of Yamaha's active monitor range. Designed for professional and project studios and for location recordists, the MSP7 has – like the NS10 – a full and forward mid-range that is superb for tracking guitars and vocals. The speakers also demonstrated the ability to track electronic bass lines very accurately.

VERDICT ★★★★★★★★☆☆

Genelec 8130A

Manufacturer **Genelec** Price **£1,222**

Contact **Source Distribution**

Web **www.genelec.com**

⬅ Like some other high-end monitoring systems, these Genelec digital input active monitors – which can be set up in stereo or surround configurations – manage to pull off a neat disappearing trick: you soon become aware that you've stopped listening to the speakers and that you're now just listening to the music. So we can't say that these speakers 'sound good' because they don't really have a 'sound' at all, which, all things considered, is probably the ultimate accolade.

VERDICT ★★★★★★★★★☆

SOUND CHOICES
Great sounding monitors to improve your mix.

KRK V6

Manufacturer **KRK Systems** Price **£598**

Contact **Focusrite 01494 462246**

Web **www.krksys.com**

→ KRK's trademark yellow woofer cone is made from woven Kevlar for its strength, lightness and rigidity. This is coupled with a 1-inch soft dome tweeter. We found the KRK V6s to be fun-sounding speakers with plenty of up-front detail, a reasonably wide soundstage and bags of bass. However, the bass was slightly sluggish with a lack of precise definition, which is fine for most rock and pop material but which wouldn't be suited to reggae or anything dubby.

VERDICT ★★★★★★★☆☆☆

M-Audio EX66

Manufacturer **M-Audio** Price **Originally £898**

Contact **M-Audio**

Web **www.maudio.co.uk**

→ M-Audio's brief for the EX66 monitors was to build "the most accurate nearfield monitors on the market" – with cost and portability secondary considerations. We were extremely impressed with the sound quality of the EX66. The imaging is outstanding, with pinpoint left/right positioning and tremendous soundstage depth. Every instrument floats in its own space, even in the most complex mixes. However, we did find the background noise generated to be higher than we would expect.

VERDICT ★★★★★★★☆☆☆

Adam A7

Manufacturer **Adam** Price **£599**

Contact **Unity Audio 01440 785843**

Web **www.adam-audio.com**

← Unlike most of the competition, the Adam A7s have the power switch and gain control on the front of the unit, so you don't have to grope around the back of your speakers, ruining all your careful alignment, whenever you want to turn them on or off. Listening to the A7s for the first time is an inspiring experience – not because of any hyped treble or artificially pumped bass, but because of their effortlessly clear and open presentation. Some ribbon-tweeter-equipped monitors can sound a little too bright and forthright, but the A7's top end is smooth and nicely proportioned.

VERDICT ★★★★★★★★☆☆

ESI nEAR 08

Manufacturer **ESI** Price **£532**

Contact **Time+Space 01837 55200**

Web **www.esi-pro.com**

← According to ESI, these monitors have been "developed to generate near-perfect sonic reproduction in any studio environment". We found we had to spend a little time getting the toe-in angle right but that the 08s delivered a solid and assured sound. Transient response is crisp, and the soft-dome tweeter has no spiky, metallic sharpness to it. We were impressed by the mid-range performance too, with vocals sounding fairly natural and present, despite a hint of flattery in the upper-mids – though things do go a awry in the low-mids and bass, where the 08s seem to over-reach themselves a bit.

VERDICT ★★★★★★★☆☆☆

MusicTech INTERVIEW

Simeon Bowring

Simeon Bowring is a busy man. There's his solo act, his electro band, a house project, a virtual mixing venture and BAFTA Award-winning video-game music. And at the centre of it all? Yep, you guessed it…

Simeon Bowring has been responsible for some truly mesmerising tunes as a solo artist (he goes by the name of Pentatonik), and some of the biggest electro beats with his band, A1 People – and he always seems to have a few other irons in the fire as well. "I've always been someone who has enjoyed the production process," he says, understatedly.

Simeon and fellow A1-er Tom Crook have brought the 'People' sound to the masses with a series of high-profile remixes – "At least 100," he estimates – including Blondie, Anastasia and Groove Armada. But two decades of

hardcore music production means that he is adept at turning his production talents to any genre, and Logic is his main tool of choice.

"I love really getting into mixing tunes and creating a sound stage and I've used Logic to do that since 2000," he explains. "A lot of my friends were using it and nearly every studio I went into had Logic. I was intrigued by the audio recording possibilities – and the plug-ins that came with it were very good. It was quite basic back in those days – computers had only just become powerful enough to make a studio in a computer possible – but I'd been using digital tape so I thought it was amazing. In fact, I still think it's amazing!"

Flexibility

"There are lots of things I like about it now," he adds. "There's the flexibility. And I like the Environment, which is still quite a big part of Logic 7, which I use. A lot of people complain about it but I like getting in there, using the arpeggiators and things like that. I also find Logic very straightforward to use. I love the plug-ins – they are very powerful – and the compressors are extremely good. The Space Designer reverb's a fantastic piece of kit. I have the impulses for a lot of extremely high-end reverbs and they just sound fantastic. I've compared the originals with the software and there's very little difference."

Simeon's Pentatonik and A1 People projects sound very different but they are linked through their use of synthesizers. We know that Simeon has a large collection ▶

SELECTED KIT LIST

- ADK Commemorative Edition Area 51 Valve Mic (with U47 tube)
- Epiphone Focusrite Liquid Mix
- M-Audio Keystation Pro 88
- MOTU Ultralite Audio Interface
- Novation Remote SL37
- PMC TB2A monitors
- SE Reflexion Filter
- Technics 1210 Turntables x2
- All Logic 7 plug-ins, NI-Spektral Delay, Nomad Factory Blueverb, Audio Damage Discord 2, Audio Damage Replicant

When he's not playing solo as Pentatonik, Simeon can often be found performing with his electro band, A1 People.

"I have the impulses for a lot of extremely high-end reverbs." SIMEON BOWRING

STEP-BY-STEP One of Simeon's favourite aspects of Logic is Capture Last Take.

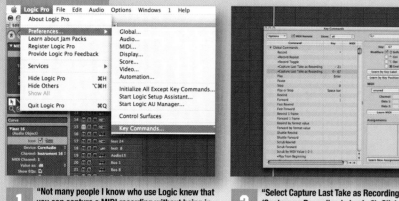

1 "Not many people I know who use Logic knew that you can capture a MIDI recording without being in record mode," says Simeon. "If you do something amazing as you jam along to the tune you can still record it even though you weren't in record mode when you played it. Select Key Commands from the Preferences menu."

2 "Select Capture Last Take as Recording in Logic 7 (Capture as Recording in Logic 8). Click on Learn by Key Position then press the key command combination you want – on my desktop I use [Shift]."

3 "Close the Key Command window. Select a MIDI track in your arrangement. Run the track (not in record). Play along, jam, etc. Press the key command combination and prepare to be amazed when what you just played appears on the screen!"

---

of hardware, but it is nowhere to be seen. Logic and software have struck again!

"The analogue synths are all in cupboards now," Simeon reveals. "I'm very much of the opinion that software synths have come of age and are in many respects better than the hardware. There's a certain joy to using hardware and my Jupiter 8 is a fantastic synth to use but you can't get it fixed now; it goes out of tune. And I don't mind using a mouse as I know what I'm doing. And I love the precision of using plug-ins, being able to call up the same settings and work on different sessions."

Simplicity

While Simeon is a fan of Logic 7's Environment he does prefer to keep things simple when he's using other aspects of the software.

"I don't use screensets, which a lot of my friends use," he says. "I tend to just flit between the Arrange page and the Mixer. But I do colour-code everything, so I tend to have my drums in dark red, guitars in green, vocals in yellow and so on. I organise everything the same way in every project so I always know where things are and am drawn to them by colour."

While Simeon uses version 7 on a day-to-day basis, version 8 is waiting in the wings to enter his production life. "I have it on my laptop and I am getting my head

around it but I've been extremely busy and haven't had a chance to learn it. What I have seen is that it is quite different, but I will go over to it eventually."

So what advice does Simeon have for the rest of us? You won't be surprised to learn that diversity is the key.

"You have to make many different styles of music. House music was something I never did but it sells well at the moment and it's also enjoyable doing something different to what you normally do. You have to be flexible, like think about making music for video games. I did some for Crackdown and we got a joint BAFTA award for that. Microsoft got the BAFTA for best use of audio, and we had a lot on there. I've also branched into mixing under the name Vertigo Heights. It's a mixing service for labels like Warners and Sony but I'm now offering my downtime to readers of magazines like this."

> "House music was something I never did but it sells well and it's enjoyable doing something different." SIMEON BOWRING

Simeon also has not one but two albums coming out on Hydrogen Dukebox Records – one each for Pentatonik and A1 People – plus a project called Stir Crazy, featuring Terry Walker on vocals, which he describes as "up-beat, main-room house music".

Finally (phew!) there's a project called The White Harts. "It's a latter day Talk Talk-type drifting thing, acoustic and folky. Even though we're using Logic, the idea is that nothing is going to be repeated so we're just playing into the software. As much as I love sequencing, it's been great getting back into the musicianship side of things. Just playing this full-size [Keystation Pro 88] keyboard has been fantastic. Two hands and actually playing something – wow!"

You can find out more about Simeon's current projects from the following websites:
www.vertigoheights.co.uk
www.myspace.com/a1people2
www.myspace.com/simeonbowring **MTF**

Simeon already has a copy of Logic 8 on his laptop but he says he's been so busy recently that he hasn't had the time to learn it yet.

Recoil Stabilizer™

Introducing the **Recoil Stabilizer™**, a unique reference monitor platform that decouples the speaker and introduces mass to provide a stable, stationary base. The principal is simple – and the results are astonishing, as these top recording engineers and producers can attest to. But don't just take their word for it... hear for yourself at aPrimacoustic dealer near you. Hearing is believing!

| **Razorblade™** quadratic diffuser | **FullTrap™** broadband absorber | **MaxTrap™** corner bass trap | **GoboTrap™** stackable absorber | **Stratus™** acoustic ceiling cloud | **Freeport™** portable gobo | **Cumulus™** mid-bass trap | **Venice™** panel system | **Australis™** corner bass trap | **Broadway™** fabric covered panels |

Shure Distribution UK, Unit2, The IO Centre, Lea Road, Waltham Abbey, Herts EN9 1AS
T : +44 (0) 1992 703058
F : +44 (0) 1992 703057
E : info@shuredistribution.co.uk

SHURE®

DISTRIBUTION UK

Using REX files in Logic Pro 8

Logic's ability to read and convert REX files is extremely useful, but sometimes the sheer number of import options may seem confusing. **Mo Volans** simplifies the task.

The release of Propellerhead's ReCycle software was a defining moment in groove-manipulation technology. The application is still being developed and remains a firm favourite with loop junkies everywhere. The REX files the program produces have been an accepted file format in numerous DAWs for some time now and you will often see entire sample libraries supplied in REX form. You may have a large REX-based library yourself, even if you have never used ReCycle to create the files.

But whether you are a seasoned ReCycle user or not, there is no denying that using REX files can be a really rewarding process and that it can greatly improve the production experience. Once inside your project you will be able to utilise the REX files' elastic audio properties and enjoy 'locked' grooves that change tempo with your project. In most cases the files also remain highly editable,

USING REX FILES CAN BE A REALLY REWARDING PROCESS AND CAN GREATLY IMPROVE THE PRODUCTION EXPERIENCE.

Power Tip

When you're using the EXS24 to play back your REX files, pay attention to the instrument's synthesis engine. Note that any envelopes used will act on each slice individually. You can achieve good acid effects with this feature, using fast filter envelopes and high resonance settings. Also try using the Drive function in conjunction with the Fat feature to saturate your loops without losing any low-end energy.

with 'slices' that can be easily moved, cut and re-arranged. And, of course, if you do own a copy of ReCycle you can take this editing process even further and create your own custom REX loops.

Most DAWs take a pretty transparent approach to their use of the REX protocol, enabling the user to import the files as if they were in any other format. Logic has a different take on proceedings and gives you several different ways in which you can import and use REX files. These different methods are all pretty straightforward in execution, but it is important that you grasp their uses if you are going to get the most out of your REX loops.

▶ If you are planning to use REX files in a similar way to how you would use raw audio files, such as WAVs or AIFFs, you will import them in a similar way. When you import them, Logic will present you with a pop-up window informing you that you are now using a file type created by Propellerhead. Click through this to reach a dropdown menu of options. These represent the different ways in which Logic can treat the incoming REX file. They break down as follows:

Crossfade
Crossfade is the default setting. This will place all the slices of your REX file onto the same track. Of course, in Logic, any overlapping audio on the same track will result in one of the files not playing back, but Logic cleverly gets around this by automatically creating a crossfade at each overlapping point.

In the initial options you will be asked for a crossfade length. Getting this right is really a matter of trial and error; different settings work with different sounds. But

once this setting is tweaked your file should play back smoothly, with all sections sounding correctly.

You will now see a single region in your Arrange window. Double-click on it and you will be taken to a new 'sub arrange' window, where you can edit the separate slices. Double-clicking outside the regions or slices will take you back to your main Arrange page.

Add Tracks
With the Add Tracks option, Logic will add a predetermined number of new tracks and place each of the new slices on its own track. The only challenge is deciding how many new tracks you create. The best way to go about this is to find out how many slices your REX file is made up of. You can do this by opening the file and manually counting the slices, or by opening it in ReCycle, if you own ReCycle.

Once your slices are on your new tracks you have accurate level control over each one and, as they are independent audio tracks, the whole file will play, ignoring overlapping parts. To edit these slices and levels double-click on the part, as you would in Crossfade mode.

Render into Single File
This is one of the most straightforward ways of importing a REX file into Logic Pro. Your file is simply converted into an untreated AIFF file. This will be totally consolidated, with no slices, and locked to the tempo of your project.

IF YOU PLAN TO USE REX FILES IN THE SAME WAY AS RAW AUDIO FILES, YOU IMPORT THEM IN THE SAME WAY.

STEP-BY-STEP Triggering a REX file via MIDI in the EXS24.

1 Create a fresh software instrument track using the Add Track icon at the top of the Arrange page. Make sure its audio outputs are set to your main stereo outs. This track will house the EXS24 soft sampler that you will use to play back your REX file.

2 Go to the software instrument track that has been created within the Logic mixer and select the EXS24 sampler from the dropdown menu. It's a good idea to use the multiple-out version as you may want to route certain slices to their own outputs.

3 Once you have opened the interface of the EXS24, load the instrument editor by clicking on the small Edit button towards the top right of the instrument. This will bring up a new floating window where you can begin to import your REX file.

4 Under the Instrument menu, go to ReCycle Convert and select the first option in the list. This will tell the editor to make a new sampler instrument, import the REX file you choose, span it across the keyboard and create and insert a matching MIDI file for playback.

5 Back to your Arrange page: you will see that a new MIDI track has been created and that the MIDI file created by the EXS24 has been inserted. This should now play back the file in the sampler. You can also inspect the notes within the MIDI region.

6 To route separate slices within the REX file to different outputs, go to the routing column in the EXS24 instrument editor, where you can designate any channel from the dropdown menu. On playback the chosen slice will fire out of the new channel.

Render into Apple Loop

Again, straightforward, but with a more flexible outcome than our previous option. Though your REX file will again be converted into one consolidated audio region, it will now be in the form of an Apple Loop. This means that although it contains no slices it has the ability to change tempo when you make changes to your project. This is possibly the most useful REX file import method here.

Don't Fix

This is actually the first option in the list but it can easily be missed. This method will simply import the REX file onto one track, slices and all. If there are any overlapping slices they will interfere with each other, so this method is only really useful when you're inspecting the slices or extracting a few sounds from a groove.

Sampling

An alternative and considerably more complex method for using REX files in Logic is to use the EXS24 as a playback device. This involves using the EXS24's instrument editor. If you are not familiar with this area of the instrument, hit Edit to bring up the appropriate screen and you can begin to find your way around.

You will notice that within the editor's Instrument menu there is a dedicated ReCycle Convert section. There are several options here that will enable you to import REX files into the EXS24 and manipulate them. You can

create MIDI parts to play back files, key-map slices and even extract specific slices for use as one-shot samples.

Using REX files in this way is useful on so many levels but the main advantages are that you can actually play the slices on a keyboard, or any other MIDI controller, and that you can use the sampler's excellent synthesis engine. The real beauty of this method lies in the fact that each slice is treated as a separate sample, so any envelopes or filters used will lock down on these individual sections independently. Using this feature you can create some really original sounds and grooves. MTF

REX Shared Library

REX Shared Library 1.6 - Universal Binary
For owners of Reason, ReCycle & Logic

Download:
Mac OS X
(If the download doesn't work, try right-clicking the link and choosing "Save link as")

This update is required to be able to use REX files created in ReCycle 2.1 with Reason 3.0 and other applications like Logic 7.2. After downloading, please mount the disk image and run the installer. This replaces the REX Shared Library with the latest version.

Note: You don't need this update if you are using Reason 3.0.5 or later.

REX Shared Library update
For owners of Reason.

Download:
Windows
Mac OS X
Mac OS 9

This update is required to be able to use REX files created in ReCycle 2.1 with Reason 2.5 and other applications. After downloading, please unpack the zip file or sit file and run the installer. This replaces the REX Shared Library with the latest version.

Note: If you have installed ReCycle 2.1 on your computer, you already have the latest REX Shared Library - there is no need to update.

What is REX?
The native ReCycle document files, REX2 files, can also be imported in a number of other programs. Space saving and efficient, they hold info about slice positions and other parameters.

For more info on using REX filess in your music, check our ReCycle pages

---

STEP-BY-STEP   Importing a REX file onto multiple audio tracks.

1 Add a new audio track using the Add Track icon at the top of the Arrange page. Whether you choose stereo or mono here will obviously depend on the format of the file you plan to use, though this can easily be changed later on if you're not sure.

2 When you have chosen the REX file you wish to import, choose the Add Tracks option from the dropdown menu. Try to make a sensible estimate of the number of tracks you need. If you do find you need more you can always undo and repeat the process.

3 You should now see a single region in your Arrange area with blocks in it representing the REX file slices that lie within. You can now trim the part or loop length to match your needs.

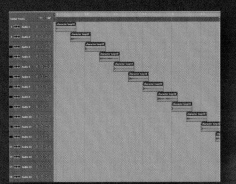

4 Double-click on this new region to reveal a 'sub arrange' page with all the slices playing back on their independent tracks. Here you can edit slices and name and organise your tracks. To return to the main Arrange page double-click anywhere outside these regions

5 When editing the slices you may notice that the mixer displays all the separate audio channels available. This is where you would add processing to a particular part. You could also create subgroups to control all or some of the individual channels

6 When you are happy with the way the part is working and it is trimmed to size, you can treat the region like any other in your arrangement and can apply edits and loops. To simplify things you can always bounce the end result into a single audio file.

ON YOUR MusicTech DVD ROM
Full-sized screenshots and all the supporting files you'll need to follow this tutorial.

LOGIC PRO 7 WORKSHOP

EXS24 DATA MANAGEMENT

Effectively managing your EXS24 files will not only improve your system's efficiency, it will also enhance your creativity. Mark Cousins delves into his hard drive.

The EXS24 is undeniably a great asset to Logic Pro, but its intricate and complex file-handling system isn't the easiest to master. And when you've installed Logic Pro 7 and all its bundled sample content you've got several hundred instruments to deal with – not to mention the thousands of samples files associated with them. It's no surprise, therefore, that many people choose to steer clear of actively organising this data, but in failing to doing so we're potentially missing out on a multitude of ways in which we can significantly improve our creative working environment.

The key to understanding and optimising the EXS24's data management is to differentiate between the various files it works with, and where these are stored on your hard drive. The two key components are the sample instruments, which contain the mapping and synthesis parameters for a sound, and the sample data, usually in the form of WAV or AIFF files, that are used to make up these instruments.

In previous versions of Logic, both these file types could be stored in Logic's Application folder – in folders

Power Tip
Do you ever find long notes on your EXS24 getting snatched off during playback? This might be due to settings in your Virtual Memory configuration and the corresponding amount of disk activity taking place. Try only activating virtual memory when you're working with big instrument files like multi-sampled pianos – and even then, try to keep disk activity, including audio tracks and QuickTime movie files, to a minimum.

THE PROBLEMS WITH SAMPLE DATA ARE THE SIZE OF THE FILES AND THE FACT THAT THEY CAN RESIDE ANYWHERE THEY WANT.

named Sampler Instruments and EXSamples respectively. In Logic Pro 7, however, things aren't quite so simple. The Sampler Instruments folder is to be found in one of two places: either in the System's Library folder – Library> Application Support>Logic>Sampler Instruments, or in your User's Library folder – mine is called MarkCousins> Library>Application Support>Logic>Sampler Instruments.

What Logic is differentiating between is user-installed or edited content, and instruments installed by Logic itself, which are technically available to all users. On loading, Logic scans both these folders – and your old Logic 6 Sample Instruments folder, if you have one – and assembles the EXS24's instrument list accordingly. **1**

Active management
Of course, there's no reason why you can't actively manage either or both of these folders, by organising instruments into different groups, by creating your own custom order for folders by adjusting the number preceding the folder's name, or by assembling folders of favourite sounds. **2**

Where are the samples? While instrument files are relatively easy to organise, the trickier task is operating with the same efficiency when you're dealing with sample data. The two big problems with sample data are the size of the files – even a 250GB drive can be filled very quickly nowadays – and the fact that they can reside anywhere they want. While this free-and-easy approach to storing sample data certainly offers a lot in terms of flexibility, it makes the job of keeping track of where your data is stored more difficult. The best solution – both for your sanity and for your computer's performance! – is to store all your sample data on a separate drive, ideally an extra SATA internal or an external FireWire drive. This way, whenever you load the Instrument, Logic simply locates the relevant files and you're ready to go. **3**

Unlinked files
In most situations, keeping your sample data on a separate drive shouldn't cause any problems. However, now and again it is possible for your instrument files and sample data to become completely unlinked – in other words, Logic can't find the files or loads the wrong samples. You might also notice that your projects take longer to load as Logic searches for the files. You could use the Project Manager window – Logic's solution for managing the full range of media and files associated with your production work – to resolve these links, but a full drive scan, especially if you have a decent-sized EXS24 library, can take several hours to complete. **4**

A much more appropriate solution for any linkage issues is Redmatica's ExsManager – you can find the demo version in the Demo Software folder on the coverdisc. As ExsManager is dedicated to working with EXS24 data, it takes far less time to scan a drive and re-link the files. In theory, even if you don't have any active linking issues, ExsManager will also make loading

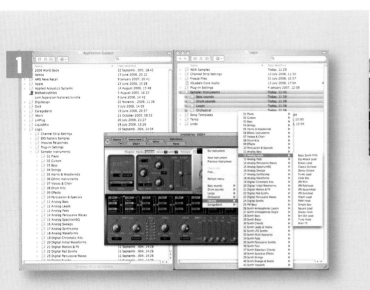

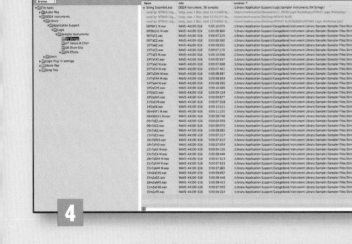

Working efficiently with the EXS24 requires active management of its instrument files and sample data. This isn't rocket science but you will need to work out the locations of the respective folders first.

far quicker, as Logic won't need to search for the sample data whenever it opens the instrument.

Song-based data

Another layer to the data management issue is song-specific EXS24 data. A good example of this is when you back up a project on completion – using File>Save As Project – and specify EXS data to be included alongside session data, audio files, plug-in settings and so on. Inside the resulting project folder you should find copies of the EXS24 instruments alongside their associated sample data. When you open the song on another computer, the EXS24 will assemble its instrument menu for both the paths we've already discussed, as well as the song's folder. Note, however, that the instruments won't be available should you open another song, as they relate only to the song folder they're saved with.

What this means is that you have effectively two choices as to where you save your EXS24 instruments: in your own Library folder, for access in subsequent projects; or in the song's folder, if you have no desire to

access the sound elsewhere and want to avoid cluttering your EXS24 instrument menu. Like many aspects of file management on modern computers, there seems to be a growing tendency to let the operating system manage everything for you. While this is fine for dealing with word processing files or family snaps, the same relaxed attitude isn't suitable for staying on top of the extreme demands of software sampling. The EXS24's data management might not be entirely transparent, but it is worth while making it fit your particular way of working.

Power Tip

OSX's Disk Management tools can help you to organise and negotiate your EXS24 data. Even simple tricks like the Labelling feature (highlight a file or folder and select File>Color Label In OSX) can help you to distinguish files. Remember that you can also drag folders to create shortcuts and so avoid the need for the rather long folder paths involved in reaching the instrument and sample folders.

LOGIC PRO 8 WORKSHOP

MATCH EQ

Match EQ is easily Logic's most powerful equalization tool and is suitable for a range of applications in both mixing and mastering. **Mark Cousins** makes his Match point.

Timbre is one of the most difficult things to get right when mixing, whether it's the track as a whole or just individual elements within the mix. Timbre can also differ between recordings – a vocal line recorded with two different microphones, for example, or different mixes sitting uncomfortably together on a finished CD. In all these situations, access to a good equalizer can help tremendously – and in that respect Logic's Channel EQ is more than suited to the task. But sometimes a lack of experience, inspiration or reliable monitoring leaves you falling short of the kind of results you want to achieve.

As an alternative to conventional equalization, Logic's Match EQ can sort out a range of timbral dilemmas, while simultaneously offering a different take on the subject. Like similar third-party products – TC Electronic's Assimilator and RNDigital's Frequal-izer, for example – Logic's Match EQ plug-in is a so-called 'intelligent' equalizer that analyses the timbre of a reference file and the existing timbre of the source, and applies a resulting spectral equalization to ideally match the two.

But how do you realistically go about using Match EQ in your productions? And can a simple equalization plug-in really be the universal panacea for the timbral issues you regularly encounter?

Match draw

One of the most obvious uses for Match EQ is as a form of mastering equalizer, whereby it assimilates the EQ characteristics of one track (usually a 'commercial' reference) and imposes them on another. However, to make sense of this match-equalization process, you need to have some stylistic and sonic parity between the two

Match EQ

tracks – don't assume that a profile gathered from a hip hop master will make any sense when applied to a guitar track!

In our first example, we're going to attempt to match two tracks: Song A – the reference track or Template – and Song B – our original master, referred to as Current Material. Both can be found in the Logic Workshop folder on the *MTF* DVD and dragged and dropped into an empty project.

For the Match EQ plug-in to work its magic, you'll need to build up spectral profiles for both the Template and Current Material. If you're working with large files this is best done as an offline process – simply [Ctrl]-click on the relevant Learn boxes to open up a Contextual menu, select Generate Spectrum Template From Audio File and choose the appropriate audio file for analysis. Alternatively, you can drag audio files directly from the Browser area onto the corresponding Learn box. 🔳

With the two files analysed, you should be able to view the corresponding frequency plots. Change the View mode from Auto to either Template or Current Material to see the frequency plots – in red and green respectively – of the two audio files. You might already be able to spot differences between the two files – a more extended top end, for example, or a deeper bass. 🔳

The Equalizer

To hear the match equalization in action, you'll need to activate the Match button for the Current Material. The Match EQ plug-in will generate a filter curve displaying any dissimilarities between the two tracks – if the source track has stronger treble, for example, you'll see a gentle

Channel EQ

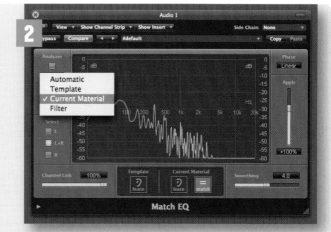

For Match EQ to work, you'll need to build spectrums for the Template (usually a source reference file, such as a commercial recording) and your Current Material (the track you want to equalize). Match EQ will create a filter curve to optimally match the Current Material to the Template.

rise in the yellow filter curve line above 5kHz. Alternatively, if your mix is overly bass-heavy, you might see a rolloff below 100Hz or so. The relative strength of this corrective equalization is established with the Apply parameter, with the best results often coming from small amounts of correction – in the region of +20% or so – rather than a complete assimilation of 100-200%. **3**

What can be hard to assess is the extent to which strong harmonic peaks – a kick drum's fundamental frequency, for example, or other prominent pitched material – will dictate the resulting filter curve. This effect is best illustrated – and modified – using the Smoothing parameter, which rounds off or sharpens the resolution of the filter curve. Reducing this to zero will show each harmonic peak clearly, but doing so often produces a corresponding sharp and edgy sound that is undesirable in most situations. **4**

Using a rounder curve (9.0 or more) will produce a more musical output, with Match EQ responding more to the overall sound rather than specific frequencies. To get the best results, look for a curve that isn't entirely dissimilar from what might be achieved with the strategic use of conventional parametric EQ, with broad cuts and boosts rather than sharp notches. **5**

Mix and Match

Although we've explored mastering applications for Match EQ, there's no reason why you can't apply it to individual sounds in the mix to match discrepancies between recordings. As an alternative to offline calculation, it's also possible to do real-time analysis simply by pressing the appropriate Learn button and running the corresponding audio material through the plug-in. If your material is on different tracks, remember that you can copy and paste spectrum profiles between Match EQ plug-ins using the same Contextual menu we initiated for the offline analysis. (The destination must be out of Learn mode to accept the spectrum profile.) **6**

Try using the Match EQ Logic project as a means of exploring these ideas in practice, taking the timbre of the piano demo track and applying it to the slightly darker finished piano. Again, aim for smother curves to pick up general timbral issues rather than specific harmonics, and make only small adjustments to avoid phase issues.

As well as smoothing, you can also impose your own equalization and adjustments to Match EQ's existing filter curve. Try adjusting the gain, especially in situations where the resulting curve has brought about some more extreme level changes. Clicking and dragging on the left

Power Tip

Although there's plenty to explore and use in Logic Pro, there are some useful features to be found in Logic's companion application, Soundtrack Pro. Use the menu feature Options>Audio>Open in Soundtrack Pro to export a region from Logic into Soundtrack Pro. One of Soundtrack Pro's best features is its Frequency Spectrum view, which provides a complete FFT plot of a file. It's also an excellent tool for audio-restoration tasks.

Match EQ is useful for helping to match two sounds within a mix. Use its copy and paste features to move spectrum templates between different instances of the plug-in. You can also edit and refine the filter's curve to achieve the type of equalization effect you're after.

MATCH EQ IS A POWERFUL AND VALUABLE EXTENSION OF LOGIC'S EXISTING EQUALIZATION FUNCTIONS.

side of the filter curve display will enable you to raise or lower the gain accordingly. You should aim for the active version of the plug-in to induce no more level than the bypassed version. [7]

Nice curves
Modifying the filter curve itself is achieved by clicking on the display and applying a reverse equalization – for example, a +5dB peak at 2kHz could be notched out with a -5dB cut. In this way, you can easily draw out peaks that you feel aren't appropriate to the effect you want to create. Pressing [Shift] enables you to change the width (or Q) of the boost. Try using wide Q settings to create a more generalised timbre lift – a shelving boost, for example – which can often sound more natural and musical than the default tight Q setting. [Alt]-clicking at any point enables you to reset the curve to its original state, including both gain modifications and extra equalization settings. [8]

More creative applications for the Match EQ plug-in involve deliberately using very different sound sources – for example, using the drums in the demo session as the Template and the piano as the Current Material. You can also achieve some interesting results using the Apply parameter in its negative setting; this will reverse the filter curve so that boosts, for example, become cuts. On the whole, though, the results rarely sound different from a dose of extreme EQ, though the process might provide a little lateral inspiration. [0]

Safety Match
For somebody with well-tuned ears and an instinctive understanding of parametric EQ, it's easy to dismiss the Match EQ plug-in as just another mixing gimmick. However, its exacting, scientific approach to the comparison of timbre can offer an illuminating insight into the timbral characteristics of a mix as a whole and of its constituent parts.

Applied sensitively, Match EQ can provide a surprising level of continuity between different sounds that even a professional engineer might struggle to achieve. And, even if you don't intend to use its output directly, you can always use Match EQ as an informative source of audio analysis, taking the information it provides and using it to determine the basic frequency and Q settings on a manually configured parametric EQ.

Either way, Match EQ is a powerful extension of Logic's existing equalization functions and a valuable means of extending your understanding and appreciation of the timbre of sound. [MTF]

Power Tip
As a quick solution for experimenting with different mastering EQs, Match EQ includes a number of pre-analysed Templates based on various genres of music, but you'll still need to carry out an analysis of your original material for Match EQ to match its curve to the properties of your track. The results can be somewhat random, but it might highlight some mix issues you hadn't thought about.

Join the Elite. Own the ELITE

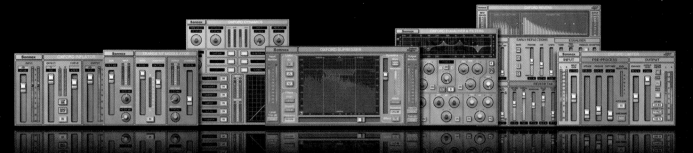

Sonnox ELITE

Ultimate Oxford Plugins Collection

Want the best sounding plug-ins available at the best possible price? Don't waste time and money collecting them one by one – save a *massive 40%* off the individual prices when buying the Sonnox ELITE collection.

All seven world renowned Oxford Plug-ins in a single bundle equates to one serious saving!.

Contains: Oxford EQ, Dynamics, Inflator, Transient Modulator, Reverb, Limiter and SuprEsser.

Mix like the pros.. join the Elite.. own the Elite.

RRP: TDM £1,825 inc. VAT   **Native £875** inc. VAT

Sonnox Essential

Loudness & Punch

If you want to mix with the same high-end plug-ins used on countless hit records all over the world - the Sonnox Essential collection has the ingredients to polish your mix. Four essential Oxford plug-ins at 30% off individual prices !

Contains: Oxford EQ, Dynamics, Reverb and SuprEsser.

RRP: TDM £1,435 inc. VAT   **Native £670** inc. VAT

Sonnox ENHANCE

Essential Mix Tools

Need that bit more? More loudness, presence, punch? The Sonnox Enhance bundle contains three simple-to-use, but incredibly powerful and loud plug-ins, to enhance your mix and give it the energy it deserves to be heard above the rest. 25% cheaper than individual prices !

Contains: Oxford Limiter, Inflator and Transient Modulator.

RRP: TDM £745 inc. VAT   **Native £375** inc. VAT

Sonnox   www.sonnoxplugins.com/bundles   **Oxford Plugins**

Pick of the plug-ins

A few well-chosen third-party plug-ins could significantly improve what you manage to achieve in Logic. **Mark Cousins** identifies some of the best options currently available.

Given the huge range of plug-ins and virtual instruments included in Logic Pro, you could easily be forgiven for wondering why you'd ever need to turn to third-party products to augment your collection. Yet while Logic's own plug-ins do cover an impressively wide range of effects and sounds, they don't quite provide us with everything that can be achieved in the virtual domain. Equally, though there are plenty of high-standard plug-ins available – such as Space Designer and the ES2 synthesizer – some don't quite cut the mustard in the more demanding professional environment, where you need to achieve release-quality results without fuss.

Indeed, throughout the years, engineers and musicians have been known to mix and match pieces of audio technology and instruments to create a richer, more diverse sonic landscape. For example, though a console might have a good on-board dynamics section – much like

Logic's own Compressor, for example – it's commonplace in a professional studio to also be able to turn to a collection of 'boutique' compressors, each bringing a different flavour – and style of compression – to the eventual mix. Equally, a sound designer will rarely use just one synth, but might have access to several different

LOGIC'S OWN PLUG-INS DON'T QUITE PROVIDE US WITH EVERYTHING THAT CAN BE ACHIEVED IN THE VIRTUAL DOMAIN.

types of synthesizers – FM, analogue subtractive, and others besides.

Over the following four pages, we're going to look at some of the best complements to the plug-ins already included in Logic, either to produce sounds and treatments that are impossible to achieve with Logic's plug-ins alone, or to take that next step in audio quality.

COMPRESSORS AND LIMITERS
How to perfect your particular flavour of squash.

1176LN

The 1176LN compressor is our favourite day-to-day mix compressor, both for its ease of use and for its versatility. The straightforward input and output controls make the compression easy to set up: simply dial in a ratio and push the input harder for more compression. The compression has a noticeable character to it, yet it's light enough on its lowest ratio setting (4:1) to suit more delicate tasks. On extreme settings – like the 20:1 ratio – the 1176LN is a great choice for 'pumpy' compression effects, especially on drums. As with all Universal Audio plug-ins, you'll need to run the 1176LN using a UAD-1 card.

Price **$149**

Download **www.uaudio.com**

X-Comp

SSL's X-Comp is one of the most interesting compressors to be released in recent years, and is arguably one of the most useful plug-ins found on its Duende system. There's lots to like about this plug-in: the transparent low-ratio compression, which works wonders across a whole mix; and some of the more extreme settings, which provide maximum squash for more abstract compression treatments. One unique feature is the ability to bleed through an amount of the HF or LF signal. This works particularly well on the high band, enabling you to restore the 'air' that other compressors can lose.

Price **£292**

Download **www.solid-state-logic.com**

L3-16

One area of weakness in Logic's plug-in collection is its Adaptive Limiter. This kind of brickwall limiting is hard to get right, so it's often worth turning to a dedicated third-party plug-in to achieve the most transparent and sonically effective results – in other words, the most loudness! Wave's latest limiter, the L3-16, follows in a long line of peak limiters that have been used in mastering studios across the world. The L3-16, though, takes the process one stage further by offering a 16-band design, potentially offering even greater loudness with unprecedented transparency across the entire audio spectrum.

Price **$900**

Download **www.waves.com**

TECHNIQUE Using the Audio Units Manager.
Making sure your plug-ins pass the basic usability test.

Logic's Audio Unit Manager works as both a plug-in validator and as a means of controlling which Audio Unit plug-ins are used by Logic. Before the Audio Unit Manager came along, Logic could be tripped up by buggy third-party plug-ins. However, by passing each plug-in through strict checks before Logic uses it, you get a more crash-free operation.

The Audio Unit Manager will run a full check of your Audio Unit plug-ins every time you run a new version of Logic for the first time, and it will update any existing profile when new plug-ins are added into your system.

For the Audio Unit Manager to do a full check can take up to 10 minutes, or perhaps even more, depending on the number of plug-ins you have installed. It's also worth remembering to make sure you've inserted all your various USB protection devices, such as iLoks and so on, as the interrogation process will effectively provoke the copy protection to check for a dongle, even though you're not actually instantiating the plug-in at this time.

Once the Audio Unit integration has completed, Logic will finish opening up. To inspect the results of the test you can open the Audio Unit Manager using the menu option Logic Pro>Preferences>Audio Units Manager.

With the Audio Unit Manager open, you can take a closer look at the plug-ins that have passed and failed validation. If a plug-in has failed, you can choose to override its being removed from your plug-ins list, though in some extreme cases you might find that this affects Logic's performance.

If a commercial plug-in fails, you'll probably find that the developer will already be aware of this and that a suitable update will have been posted on their website.

Occasionally, it is possible for a plug-in to slip through the Audio Unit validation process, or not even be scanned. In this situation, click on the Reset and Rescan option to manually prompt the Audio Unit Manager to revalidate your plug-in folder accordingly.

You can use the Audio Unit Manager to re-establish any plug-ins that might have failed the validation process, though you might experience some stability issues with Logic.

EQUALIZERS

Tools with which to polish the timbre of your mix.

Oxford EQ

Sonnox's Oxford Equalizer, which is ported from the same code used in Sony's OXF-R3 console, is one of the best workhorse equalizers currently available. If you're used to Logic's Channel Equalizer, then you'll soon be able to adapt to the Oxford EQ because of its fully parametric, five-band design. This is a great-sounding EQ, capable of pulling the mix together in a truly effective way, while at the same time not overstating its presence. The different curve types also enable you to assimilate certain qualities of famous EQs, such as those from Neve, SSL or Pultec.

Price **£200**

Download **www.sonnoxplugins.com**

1073 EQ

This is another great plug-in from Universal Audio's UAD-1 system, modelling one of the best-respected equalizers used in recording: the Neve 1073, as originally featured on the 8014 console. Though nowhere near as flexible as Logic's Channel Equalizer, the 1073 Neve EQ exudes a musicality that few plug-in equalizers can match, making it an excellent choice for sweetening activities – like a 12kHz treble boost, for example – or where you need some light control in the mids. Just don't expect anything too flexible: there are only six frequency steps to play with!

Price **$249**

Download **www.uaudio.com**

PuigTec EQP-1A

The original Pultec EQP-1A is a real studio stalwart and several plug-in versions have now been created. The latest version is Waves' PuigTec EQP-1A, available as part of the new JJP Collection bundle. Like the original, the PuigTec EQP-1A is vastly different to Logic's fully parametric equalizer, with just two bands of equalization and a high-frequency attenuator to play with. This plug-in is all about character, though, thanks to the wide bell of the high-frequency control and the ability to apply both a cut and a boost to the low frequencies at the same time.

Price **$800 (as part of the JJP Collection)**

Download **www.waves.com**

SYNTHESIZERS

Top synth tools for all your sound design requirements.

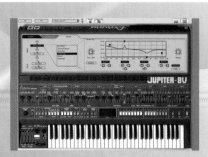

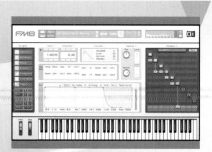

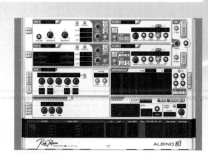

Jupiter-8V

Arturia has developed a range of software synths modelled on the hardware classics – including the CS-80V and Minimoog V – but it's the Jupiter-8V that most people seem to turn to on a regular basis. Much easier to understand than the ES2, the Jupiter-8V can produce a range of classic subtractive sounds – from deep basses to warm and luscious pads – with plenty of presets to get you up and running. More contemporary features, such as the Galaxy modulator and the flexible effects engine, help keep the Jupiter-8V bang up to date, making this synth just as useful for cutting-edge sound design.

Price **£169**

Download **www.arturia.com**

FM8

Although Logic includes its own FM Synthesizer – the EFM1 – this comes nowhere near the flexibility and sonic dexterity of Native Instruments' FM8. With up to six conventional operators, plus distortion and analogue filter operators, the FM8 can produce everything from icy pads to woofer-shaking synth basses, as well as many of the classic sounds produced by Yamaha's original DX7. The patch-morphing controls also enable you to create plenty of unique sounds, often with quite unexpected results, and the timbre of FM synthesis makes the FM8 output quite distinct from that of other examples.

Price **£169**

Download **www.native-instruments.com**

Albino 3

Rob Papen's Albino might not exactly break the mould when it comes to cutting-edge synthesis techniques, but a strong range of intelligent features – such as a step sequencer, arpeggiator, and some gutsy-sounding filters – make this a synthesizer that you'll want to come back to time after time. Having programmed many of the presets for leading hardware synths – such as the Access Virus – the 2,000 or more sounds included with the Albino 3 cover a good range of contemporary synthesizer sounds, many of which are specifically aimed at specific genres, such as drum'n'bass and trance.

Price **£129**

Download **www.robpapen.com**

DRUMS AND PERCUSSION
Cutting-edge plug-ins for a range of rhythmic effects.

BFD2

If you're after a natural acoustic drum sound then FXpansion's BFD2 has to be one of the best options currently available on the market. The drums themselves have been sampled in meticulous detail, with up to 96 different velocity levels filling a whooping 55GB of hard drive space. As with the original BFD, you'll also find room mics, inside and outside kick mics, and snare top and bottom mics, enabling you to mix and match the elements – alongside BFD2's compression, equalization, and other effects – to produce a release-quality output that is almost indistinguishable from a real kit.

Price **£235**

Download **www.fxpansion.com**

Stylus RMX

As you'd expect, Spectrasonics' Stylus RMX is a real treasure chest of contemporary loops, from dirty, compressed breakbeats right though to cutting-edge electronica. Although it's easy to be impressed by just the loops alone, the real star has to be Spectrasonics' Advanced Groove Engine (SAGE), which enables the loops to be manipulated, time-stretched, and processed far beyond their original musical purpose. Even better still, you can also import any other third-party REX files – or your own audio files processed via ReCycle – into Stylus RMX, making it one of the most flexible REX players available.

Price **£169**

Download **www.spectrasonics.net**

Battery 3

Logic's Ultrabeat is certainly a good starting place if you're interested in programming your own drum breaks from scratch, but the wealth of sound content (totalling 12GB) that is included in Battery 3 will make this an excellent addition to your plug-in folder. Also, unlike Ultrabeat's interface, Battery 3's clear, cell-based mapping system makes the process of creating kits an intuitive exercise, with effects such as compression, EQ and reverb all easy to apply on a drum-by-drum basis. And for even more sound content, remember to check out Native Instruments' excellent Synthetic Drums 2 sound library.

Price **£169**

Download **www.native-instruments.com**

STEP-BY-STEP Automating the parameters of your plug-ins.

1 Automating the parameters of your plug-ins can really help bring your effects to life – whether it's moving the cutoff of a filter or the regeneration of a delay line. To automate your parameters, engage the Automation view [A] and put the track into Touch mode.

2 Touch mode should be your default setting for recording or replacing automation data. Once you've started the transport, all you need to do is move the corresponding parameter on the plug-in and Logic will begin recording the moves.

3 Once you release the controls in Touch mode, the recording will stop, though the transport will continue to play, of course. To replace any of the moves, simply grab the controls at the appropriate point in the track and Logic will replace your data.

4 If you need to display more than one track of automation data – maybe you're automating two parameters, for example – you can always use the arrow at the bottom of the track list to open up another track lane for you.

5 As well as writing in moves by hand, you can also use the Arrange window's tools to edit existing automation data, or even draw in completely new moves. Try using the Marquee tool as a means of selecting and duplicating a series of moves.

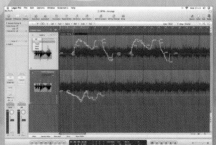

6 If you decide later on that you want to soften the overall settings, use the [Apple] key and click on the small automation meter to globally trim the level accordingly. When you're done, return the track to Read mode to prevent accidental deletion.

REVERB AND DELAY
Better ways to increase the spaciousness of your mix.

Altiverb 6

Although Logic's own Space Designer is a fantastic convolution-based reverb, it can fall short in respect to the quality and diversity of the IR profiles that are included with it. Sometimes more is required. Now in its sixth incarnation, Audio Ease's Altiverb has been steadily building up an impressive library of real acoustic spaces – such as the Fox Scoring Stage and the Notre Dame Cathedral, for example – as well as the best in synthetic reverbs, from vintage EMT Plate Reverbs owned by Wendy Carlos through to the classic AMS and Lexicon digital reverbs that were so favoured by sound engineers in the 1980s.

Price £410

Download **www.audioease.com**

Roland RE-201

If you're already a fan of Logic's own Tape Delay plug-in, then you're going to just love the effects you can achieve with Universal Audio's Roland RE-201, a faithful recreation of the classic Space Echo effect. Even more grungy and lo-fi than Tape Echo, the Roland RE-201 not only delivers delay and reverb effects but, thanks to the crunched-up return, it also adds distinct tone and timbre that will lend significant body and interest to your mix. For experimental purposes at least, try automating the intensity control to recreate the classic regenerative delay so commonly used in dub and trip hop.

Price $199

Download **www.uaudio.com**

CSR

If you want to avoid the CPU drain of convolution reverb, you're not left with a great amount of choice in Logic. Platinum Reverb, though good in its time, doesn't really stand up to close scrutiny, often producing a somewhat grainy or metallic output. Some of the better third-party modelled reverbs, such as IK Multimedia's CSR, produce a far more audiophile output, creating wide, luscious reverbs without taxing your CPU usage greatly. Though less realistic than a convolution reverb, this is a good modelled reverb that sits well in the mix, often producing a less cluttered low end than an acoustically-sourced reverb.

Price €329

Download **www.ikmultimedia.com**

THE BEST OF THE REST
Essential plug-ins no Logic user should be without!

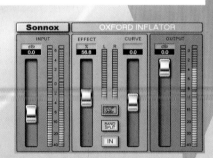

Guitar Rig 3

While Logic's Guitar Amp Pro concentrates on the simple combination of amp, cabinet and microphone, Native Instruments' Guitar Rig 3 provides you with a complete guitar rig, full of effects, amplifiers, microphones and so on. The output of Guitar Rig is surprisingly authentic, producing results that would require several thousand pounds' worth of hardware to create outside of the computer. However, it is also equally adept at a range of lo-fi treatments in the mix, providing some soft-speak colouration on a drum loop, for example, or some extreme distortion across a vocal line.

Price £229

Download **www.native-instruments.com**

Melodyne plug-in

Originally, the Melodyne was only available as a separate application, but the move to incorporate Celemony's innovative pitch-and-time manipulation technology into a plug-in has brought a whole new level of versatility to Logic. Once the audio has been scanned into an instantiation of Melodyne, you can freely manipulate the pitch and time of your music, which is ingeniously represented as a series of blobs. Of course, Melodyne comes into plenty of good use when you're fixing vocal tuning problems, but there's also a wealth of further creative potential that's just waiting to be discovered!

Price £249

Download **www.celemony.com**

Oxford Inflator

Loudness is usually associated with heavy compression: the aggressive squashing of transients to produce a mix with a greater amount of RMS energy and a more consistent peak level. Though brickwall limiters offer a quick solution for this process, they often leave you with a mix that has lost its percussive bite and dynamic range. Sonnox's Inflator achieves the feat of increasing loudness without inducing compression-like artefacts. Given its approach, the results are impressive, making the Inflator an excellent way of adding a touch of 'size' and impact to anything you choose to pass through it.

Price £115

Download **www.sonnoxplugins.com**

LOGIC PRO 7 WORKSHOP

CREATING A SCORE

Creating a complete score from a MIDI sequence in Logic Pro doesn't require a degree in music theory. **Mark Cousins** swaps his manuscript paper for a mouse.

One of the key original concepts behind Logic Pro – dating back to its initial release as Notator Logic in 1993 – was that score editing should be an integral part of the sequencing process. Notator Logic was designed as a system that integrated with the composition process, enabling scores to be composed, sequenced and printed from a single computer. And in its latest incarnation, Logic's score-editing tools make it easy to turn instrumental doodlings into music that real people can play – and all with a minimal understanding of music theory.

In this workshop we're going to look at the process of turning sequenced material into a finished arrangement – adapting the sequence to make it playable, and preparing both the full score and individual parts for the various players. We will start with a basic keyboard part, which you'll find on the coverdisc, and we're going to adapt it for a four-piece string ensemble.

The first task is to split the polyphonic performance into four monophonic parts that the string players can work with. Take the sequence into the Matrix editor and

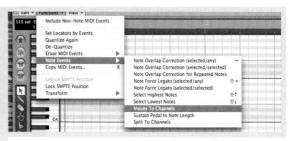

However, what should be immediately apparent is that each instrument is incorrectly displayed in a traditional piano stave – that is, as two lines of music for the left and right hands. Try selecting each of the parts and changing its display parameters to something more appropriate. The violins, for example, should be set to Treble; the viola to Viola; and the cello to Bass. Note how the staves and clefs change accordingly. **3**

With the basic clefs and staves configured, let's make some further refinements to make the score even more readable and – most importantly – musically expressive. To avoid having too many sharps or flats littering the score – and to help your musicians identify the key of the piece – you'll need to set the key signature of the score. Click on the small collection of flats – denoted by the symbol – in the Part box and select the Dm key from the top of the Score Objects box, sliding it across onto the clef. The key of the score is now set and the resulting score will be much easier to read. **4**

Adding expression

Following the same process we used to establish the key of the score, we can now drag our musical expression markings – dynamics, crescendos, diminuendos and so on – to add further interest and colour to the arrangement. Double-clicking on the Dynamics symbol in the Part box – indicated by the letters 'fp' – will bring up a floating palette of dynamics markings. These can be dragged onto the score and placed underneath a note as required. Try doing the same with the crescendo and diminuendo markings to add a rise and fall in volume at particular points in the score. Note that the diminuendo and crescendo expression markings contain handles that enable you to control their duration. **5**

Use the Text tool to insert the song's title at the top of the score and you should be ready to start printing the finished manuscript. To fit the entirety of the music on as few pages as possible, you can afford to shrink the percentage scaling of the score. To do this, go to

LOGIC'S SCORE-EDITING TOOLS MAKE IT EASY TO TURN INSTRUMENTAL DOODLINGS INTO MUSIC THAT REAL PEOPLE CAN PLAY.

check for any notes that exceed four voices. Delete these extra notes, ensuring that the musicality of the original part isn't too badly affected. **1**

By pressing the [Shift] key and the Up and Down arrows you can select the top or the bottom line of the part. By toggling the selection ([Shift]+T) you can remove unwanted notes, leaving just a single musical line. Do copy the part before you delete any notes – ideally with the line selected so you know what you've removed – so you're slowly filtering from the bottom to the top, or vice versa. Assigning the edits to four consecutive instances of EXS – with the tracks named appropriately: Violin I, Violin II, Viola and Cello – will also enable you to audition the rationalisation that is taking place. **2**

Preparing the score

To prepare the full score, select all the parts and open the Score editor. You should see an Instrument Set – this is Logic's collective name for a number of instrumental parts displayed in a score – and a layout that is representative of the finished piece of music.

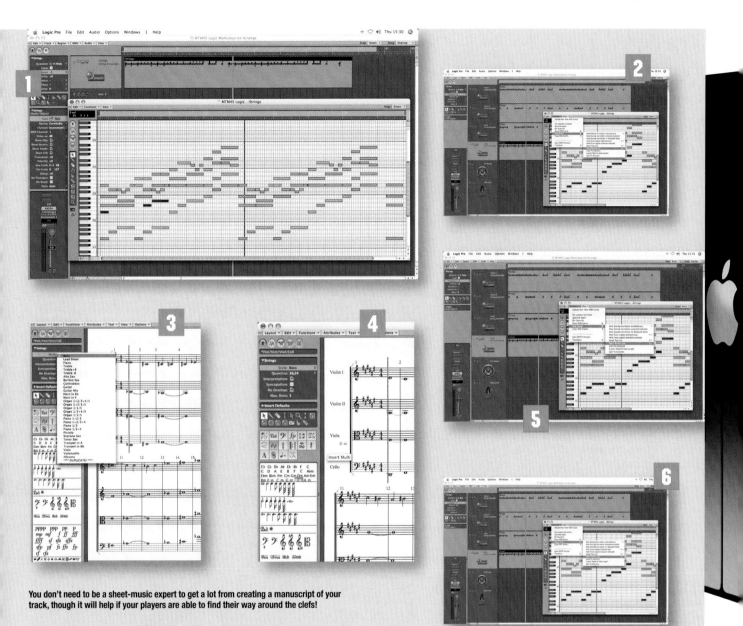

You don't need to be a sheet-music expert to get a lot from creating a manuscript of your track, though it will help if your players are able to find their way around the clefs!

Layout>Instrument Sets and adjust the Scale (%) parameter to around 70%. You can print the parts by double-clicking on any of the instrumental lines, which will take you down to part level – click on a blank part to return to the full score. For parts, you'll probably want to print at 100% scaling, so re-adjust the Instrument Set accordingly before printing. 6

Energy and life

Despite the temptation to use virtual instruments all the time, there's a surprising amount of extra value that can added to a piece of music by using real musicians. In this respect, Logic Pro's score-editing features are essential to unlocking a whole world of music beyond the confines of the virtual domain. Even something as simple as expression markings can transform the energy and life of a piece of music in ways that are either tremendously time-consuming or effectively impossible to achieve with samples alone. The Score editor isn't just another means of editing MIDI data, but a completely different way of making music. MTF

THERE'S A SURPRISING AMOUNT OF EXTRA VALUE THAT CAN BE ADDED TO A PIECE OF MUSIC BY USING REAL MUSICIANS.

Power Tip

One really convenient way to create and archive scores is to use the built-in PDF-authoring functions of OSX, which can be accessed under the PDF button for OSX's Print options. Saved as a PDF file, you can spend time getting the score to look right, and then print off the pages as required. Of course, a PDF file is also easy to email to players, so this is a great way to prepare the players ahead of the session itself!

"The tracks went down onto ADAT so we're trying to find one of those at the moment."
ANDY ORGAN, BOMBAY MONKEY

MusicTech INTERVIEW

Bombay Monkey

Bombay Monkey are rising stars on the UK music scene and use Logic to help produce their unique sound, but they have a rather refreshing outlook that mixes the best of both old and new compositional methods.

ombay Monkey are one of the brightest names in underground music today, with an outlook and style that is getting them noticed in all the right circles. They have just released their third album, 130 Astronauts, in what they call 'a trilogy of four parts'. This follows Vanish (released in 2005) and Time Travelers (2006). Their style is chilled, cinematic, enigmatic, retro – and perhaps a little kitsch. If it sounds like we're having trouble labeling them, check out the Istanbul Dub excerpt on their MySpace page – it has a little bit of everything!

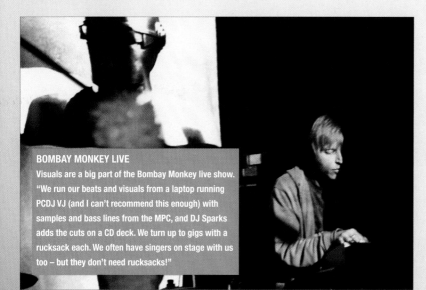

BOMBAY MONKEY LIVE
Visuals are a big part of the Bombay Monkey live show. "We run our beats and visuals from a laptop running PCDJ VJ (and I can't recommend this enough) with samples and bass lines from the MPC, and DJ Sparks adds the cuts on a CD deck. We turn up to gigs with a rucksack each. We often have singers on stage with us too – but they don't need rucksacks!"

"I was working as a producer and engineer at S16 Studios when Bombay Monkey formed in 2002," recalls the band's Andy Organ. "We met up through the hip hop label Defcon. Guy Martin [the other Monkey] shared a flat with two of the rappers he was building beats for at S16 and he came by for an afternoon to learn about Cubase and we ended up building a track there and then. We started working together regularly – mostly in the same flat (130 St John's Rd, Tunbridge Wells – hence the title of 130 Astronauts) – about a year later."

Back then, as well as using Cubase, the duo used MiniDisc for recording audio and an Akai MPC2000. Their first break came through working with DJs 1st Rate and Mr Thing and they have since worked with many UK rappers and other bands.

"We ended up getting our own music released through a friend who works at Canadian label Nettwerk's UK offices," says Andy. "He's always been into what we do and sorted out a distribution deal for us."

And what of this trilogy in four parts? What's to come after the release of 103 Astronauts?

"We're about to start work on Prophecy Of, which is the prequel to the first three albums," Andy explains. "We booked into a studio to record the vocals on this back in 2003 and the tracks went down onto ADAT so we're trying to find one of those at the moment. Hopefully it won't turn into the equivalent of *The Phantom Menace* now we've got decent kit to mix it on!"

Despite once saying that computers should be avoided when making music, Bombay Monkey succumbed to the inevitable when they were introduced to Logic through other producers and studios.

STEP-BY-STEP Creating project templates and saving time.

1 Andy considers Project Templates a must-use feature in Logic. When you load a new project you have the choice of a few preset templates that might be useful. Here we've loaded Instruments, which has 'a diverse selection of instruments from Logic's library'. Very nice, but you can create your own too. To save a project template, use the option on the dropdown file menu – but there's more to creating a logical template than that.

2 A good idea is to create a MIDI and Audio template to give you maximum flexibility. Load in some of your favourite instruments and effects on each channel, but try to avoid the processor-hungry ones or your template might reach the CPU ceiling before you've even recorded a note! We've set our favourite instruments across the instrument channels and some commonly used effects across the audio channels. Easy, but there's more…

3 Click on the Settings icon at the top of any channel strip to save all the settings – instruments, effects, parameters and so on – for another project. Here we've saved our favourite channel instrument as 'fave instrument'. To load that into another project, open that project, click on the Media icon (top right in Logic) and select Library. Click on the Setting icon of the channel you want it to replace and it will appear in the dropdown menu.

"Everyone we'd come across in the industry seemed to be using Logic," says Andy, "As an aspiring production team we had to be compatible so we bought our first copy, version 5. This definitely turned out to be a good call: most people we work with pass on Logic files."

Earlier versions of Logic were often regarded as being difficult to learn, but Andy and Guy didn't find this at all. "One of the best things about Logic was how painless it is to learn," says Andy. "We didn't want a writing tool: we wanted a really good arranging, recording and mixing tool; it's helped me to separate the writing and recording processes. While you can complete a track from start to finish on a computer, it's easy to get distracted into mixing your music before you've actually got your music."

That's a very good point – and one that we could all learn from. Andy goes on to reveal that Bombay Monkey don't use Logic for the writing stage at all, preferring a more traditional route.

The heart of the music

"Logic is at the heart of our studio but it's not the heart of our music," he states. "All our tracks start life with a stack of old records and an Akai MPC2000. If you're looking for a fast, easy way to get something cooking, it's unbeatable. Around the time we were building our studio, a whole batch of friends seemed to be doing the same. I'd often get

The Bombay Monkey live show mixes up their music with live scratching and video clips from cult TV shows and cartoons.

asked to check out someone's setup and, for me, the acid test was: 'Can you record from a record deck?' Anyone using PCs ran into trouble: they couldn't get a signal in or they couldn't access the file in Cubase or Acid or whatever software. An hour later maybe half of them had solved the problem but all of them had lost the moment."

So the Akai and a record deck capture 'the moment' but Logic is used to arrange and mix the results. "It's like having a brilliant hi-fi," says Andy, "and you don't think about it unless something breaks, but it just doesn't break – and credit to Macs here too because they don't break."

> "We didn't want a writing tool: we wanted a really good arranging, recording and mixing tool." ANDY ORGAN

With Logic providing arranging and mixing duties, it's no surprise to hear Andy citing its effects and editing functions as being among his favourite features. "Copy and pasting EQ or effects parameters and looped recording," he replies when asked what features he uses most. "I love all the automation too. Any time you need to move any parameter, Logic can learn it. Brilliant!"

When asked what they would like to see improved, Andy admits that they are still on version 6, but not for long… "We just did some music for an ice-cream commercial that's going out in various eastern European countries and version 8 is on the shopping list when we get paid!" he laughs. "On version 6 the MIDI grid edit is still fiddly. Also, I can't seem to record MIDI instruments and audio at the same time."

So what top tips have they picked up from using Logic? Three, as it turns out: make templates for projects; take frequent breaks; work on tracks in batches of three." Andy counts these off before offering some more general advice for music production.

"Try and avoid using presets or sample libraries," he suggests. "Work quickly and don't miss the moment because you've been experimenting with a plug-in. Keep tracks short: say what you gotta say then stop!" MTF

SELECTED KIT LIST
- Apple Mac G5 running Logic with two MOTU 828s
- Rode NT1A and NT2A mics
- AKG and Shure SM58 / SM57s mics
- Allen and Heath GS3000 with two valve pre-amps
- Yamaha NS10 and Alesis M1 (Mk2) monitors
- Akai MPC 2000 and S900 samplers
- Carillon controller keyboard

COMPLETE YOUR COLLECTION!

Expanding Logic with ReWire

Some of the best ways to expand the capabilities of Logic involve using ReWire-savvy applications and distributed processing. **Mo Volans** shows you how to share the load.

xpanding the sonic capabilities of Logic can be readily achieved simply by purchasing hardware synthesizers, outboard processors or DSP-driven FX. While all of these are perfectly valid ways of expanding your setup, they are all obviously expensive and there is a possibility that you may lose the convenience of your 'in the box' setup. With extra outboard comes extra wiring and in turn a larger interface or mixing console. The instant recall you are so used to could also be lost if you choose this route.

Before you splash out on extra kit, or even a new computer, it's worth looking closer to home for an alternative path. Many of us don't realise it but we may already have the resources we need to create an expanded Logic system without breaking the bank or losing any recall ability.

THIS MEANS THAT AN INJECTION OF NEW SOUNDS MAY BE JUST AROUND THE CORNER.

ReWire behavior: [Live Mode (Higher CPU Load)]

Power Tip

No matter how many ReWired applications, channels and instruments you are using, Logic can automatically calculate the correct amount of delay compensation, so everything stays in time. Of course, as you add more to your project the latency may become intrusive to your recording and playing. By changing ReWire's behaviour in Logic's Audio Preferences to Live mode, you can cut this latency, though your CPU load will increase.

Every DAW supplies different instruments and processors that are often exclusive to that package. For instance, even though you may want to, you can't use a plug-in or instrument from Reason directly in Logic's Environment, or vice versa. Yet though these plug-ins are locked to their parent applications, there is a method that enables you to route audio between certain applications. It involves using the ReWire protocol.

ReWire was a joint development by Swedish software company Propellerhead and the German powerhouse Steinberg. It came out in 1998 as part of Propellerhead's (now discontinued) classic ReBirth TB-303 emulator ReBirth. ReWire's original purpose was simply to route audio from a few select Propellerhead products to Cubase SX, but the protocol proved hugely popular and after years of use it is now an industry-standard method of streaming audio between applications.

Most music-production platforms use the ReWire protocol and can communicate with other systems, either as a host or as a slave. What this means is that an injection of new sounds may be just around the corner. If you ▶

▶ own more than one DAW, coupling them via ReWire could give you access not only to extra instruments and processors but also to any other features that the secondary application may offer.

As an example of this feature sharing, imagine a project that has been recorded and constructed in Logic, using its extensive mixing capabilities, and then ReWired with Ableton Live to utilise that DAW's elastic audio capabilities and real-time loop triggering. Not only can audio from other applications be routed directly into Logic's mixer but the integration is deep enough so that

WHEN THIS HAPPENS YOU MAY THINK THAT THE ONLY OPTION IS TO SHELL OUT FOR A MORE POWERFUL COMPUTER.

MIDI channels and specific instruments can be selected from within Logic. Any MIDI you wish to input can then be played in Logic, rather than the slave application.

Routing for you

If you're using an application as a ReWire slave, you will need to start Logic Pro first, and then the application you want to slave to it. This ensures that the slave application's audio is correctly routed through ReWire to Logic. When you shut down the applications, you will need to reverse

this process; failing to quit the programs in the correct order will result in a helpful on-screen prompt. This sounds like an unnecessary noodle, but once you've done it a few times it becomes second nature.

With the two applications loaded and ReWired you should see some kind of confirmation of the link in the slave program – in Reason 4, for example, the Audio Interface device at the top of the rack will tell you that you are now in ReWire Slave mode. You are now ready to start routing your audio signals into Logic.

Within Logic you can now create auxiliary audio channels in the Environment and select the ReWired outputs from your slave application for use as inputs. The audio will now stream into Logic as if it were playing back from an internal audio track. Both Logic and third-party plug-ins can be applied to the stream in the normal way and the resulting audio can even be bounced and exported within Logic.

Using MIDI instruments across a ReWire connection simply involves creating a new ReWire object in the Environment. You can now select any of the instruments within the active Reason project using the Library section of Logic's media browser. These Reason devices can now be played as if they were Logic instruments. You can also use MIDI-controller signals to automate your movements of instrument parameters.

It is quite likely that once you start to use this method

STEP-BY-STEP **Using Reason instruments via ReWire.**

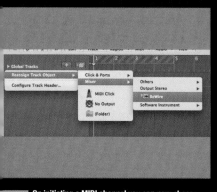

1 With Logic open and your project loaded, open Reason. Reason will automatically sense that there is another ReWire application open and go into ReWire Slave mode. This much is indicated by the readout on Reason's audio interface device at the top of the rack.

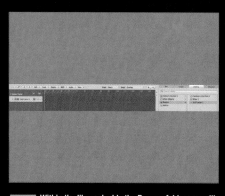

2 Create a mixer and an instrument of your choice. Make sure that the mixer's main output is routed to the first two channels of Reason's audio interface. These should be illuminated in green to indicate that they are available and active ReWire input channels.

3 Back in Logic, create a new ReWire object within the Environment. The object will look different to the other channels – auxiliaries and busses, etc. You will still be able to select it and edit its values in the Inspector to the left of the Environment's interface.

4 On initiating a MIDI channel you can now choose Reason as your destination object by 're-assigning the track object'. This is a global selection and will not be directed at any particular instrument, so don't worry if you don't hear or see any evidence of the link.

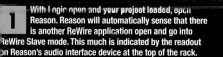

5 Within the library inside the Reason folder you will see a list of available destinations. Select the instrument you created in Reason – in this case a Subtraktor synth. You can now trigger the instrument with your input device. There is a MIDI light on the front panel

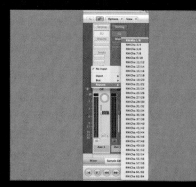

6 To route Reason's audio into Logic, create an aux channel in the Environment and select Reason's first two channels as its input. In Logic's mixer you can now see – and hear – incoming audio from the instrument in Reason. This can be treated like any audio

for playing instruments from other applications, you will soon need more than the basic single stereo that is supplied by using one auxiliary channel. If this is the case, simply enable more ReWire outputs in the slave application and add more auxiliary channels in Logic. You can also duplicate the MIDI channels and assign them to new instruments. Using this technique you can construct a true multi-channel, multi-timbral platform spanning two or more DAWs.

CPU load

When you're using slave applications with Logic your scope for sound creation is greatly enhanced but with this extra freedom comes greater CPU load. Fortunately, any extra weight on your CPU is displayed centrally in Logic's performance meter, so you can quickly see what your remaining resources are.

Of course, with all this extra processing taking place it may not be long before your beloved studio machine folds under the pressure and your project comes to a grinding halt. When this happens you may think that the only option is to shell out for a more powerful computer, but it is likely that there is much cheaper alternative.

If you have an old Mac lying around, or if you have access to one, you can take advantage of a Logic feature called Distributed Processing. This involves using a small application called a Logic Node on each machine you

Power Tip

You don't have to limit yourself to just one host and one slave when using ReWire applications; the ReWire protocol is more than capable of handling multiple applications at once, as is Logic Pro. Maybe you've imagined using the looping capabilities of Ableton Live in conjunction with the instruments and effects in Reason's rack, all mixed in Logic. This is now easily achievable, and with Logic 8's updated ReWire integration, setting things up is a breeze.

want to you use. Once the machines are linked via ethernet, processing duties for audio units can be shared between the processors on each machine. The node is displayed as a new bar in the performance meter so you can keep a track of things. Although ReWire channels – and any other aux or busses – can't yet be processed using nodes, you should find that you free up plenty of extra CPU using this feature. This will enable you to run much larger projects. MTF

STEP-BY-STEP   Using special FX to twist a vocal part.

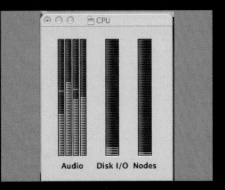

1 Make sure you have Apple's Logic Node application installed on all the machines you wish to use in your distributed processing network. It should be in your applications folder if you have already installed Logic Pro. If you can't find it you can get it off the Logic Install DVD.

2 Open the Node application on both (or all) machines. It is extremely important that the version of the Node application is the same on all machines in the network. Connect the computers via Gigabit Ethernet and enable file-sharing across the board.

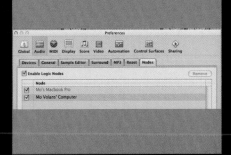

3 In Logic's Preferences select the Nodes tab in the Audio section. Tick the Enable Nodes box and also tick any machines in the network you want to use. Core audio will now restart and enable the network.

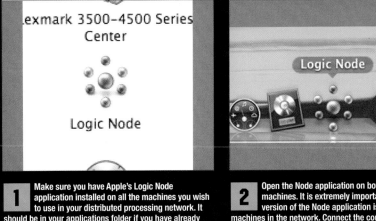

4 Node buttons are now available on your audio tracks. Activate some of them to test the connections. If they turn green, you're good to go; if you get a flashing broken line or a greyed-out symbol the connection was unsuccessful. Check your connections.

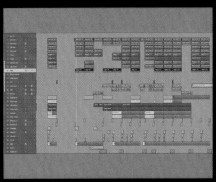

5 You should now be able to see an extra bar appear in your Performance Meter, labelled Nodes. You can keep an eye on how much processing the network is doing here – you should see the benefits as your native CPU level drops.

6 With everything swimming along smoothly you should now be able to run many more tracks live and really feel a considerable performance boost. This extra headroom can give you the room to run more instruments, effects and ReWire channels.

LOGIC PRO 8 WORKSHOP

EXS24 INSTRUMENT EDITOR

Conquering the EXS24 Instrument Editor will enable you to fully exploit the potential of Logic's supreme software sampler. **Mark Cousins** reveals the secrets of this upgrade.

One of the most overdue improvements in Logic Pro 8 has been the introduction of an updated version of the EXS24 Instrument Editor. As an integral part of the application, the EXS24 is arguably one of Logic's most useful day-to-day production tools, offering a powerful suite of sampling tools to rival the likes of Kontakt or GigaStudio. The new Instrument Editor certainly makes sample mapping a far quicker and more intuitive task, though some of the finer aspects of the EXS24 operation – particularly with respect to the interaction between the editor and the main interface – can take some time and patience to fully understand.

Most people's initial encounter with the EXS24 will be via the main plug-in window – also known as the Parameters window – which is principally used as a means of navigating the EXS24's instruments, as well as modifying the key sound parameters – filter settings, ADSR envelopes and so on – of the currently loaded instrument. If you want to delve deeper, the EXS24 Instrument Editor enables you to build complex mappings and triggering options for samples organised across the keyboard. Of course, this audio data can either come from the session itself – dragged directly from the Audio Bin – or be imported from an alternative source, such as a disc of samples.

Opening up
You can open the EXS24 Instrument Editor with the small Edit tab in the top right corner of the EXS24 plug-in window. You'll see a screen that has been divided up into a number of different areas to facilitate data navigation and mapping within your instrument. One of the key points to note at this stage is the difference between the Zone and Groups views – both of which are selectable

using the tabs in the top left corner. The Zone view contains the mapping details of individual samples across the keyboard; the Groups view enables you to deal with macro information within an instrument, grouping together related zones – such as those relating to a given range of velocities, for example – so that they can be handled in a common way. 1

Importing samples
Unless you're starting from an adaptation of an existing EXS24 instrument, you'll need to select New from the Instrument menu to create an initialised instrument to work with. Sample data can be imported into the Instrument Editor in a number of different ways. The first option is to use the Zone menu – either to create new empty zones into which samples can be assigned, or by using the Load Multiple Samples menu option, if you have a number of samples that need to be spread across the keyboard. If you use the Load Multiple Samples option, Logic will present you with a number of auto-mapping options: Auto Map, which uses the root key embedded in the audio file name; Drums, which again uses the root key from the audio file but which adjusts several zone parameters to optimise the mapping for drums; and Contiguous Zones, which creates a stream of zones irrespective of file naming. 2

If you prefer a manual, drag-and-drop approach to building up your mapping, you can always use a combination of the Audio Bin and the Browser within Logic to build instruments by hand. What's interesting to note, though, is the different ways the samples can be mapped, based on where you drag them to on the editor. For example, dragging the samples down directly onto the keyboard on the bottom of the editor will assign them to a single corresponding key; drag them towards the Zone list and the sample will be mapped across the full range of the keyboard. Note that you can also drag multiple samples across directly from the Browser or the Audio Bin, with Logic prompting for you for an appropriate auto-mapping solution. 3

With either approach, though, it's important to keep your samples in an appropriate location on your hard drive so that Logic can find the data again. (For more information on the best locations for keeping samples, take a look at the EXS24 Data Management workshop in this magazine.)

Zone parameters
As well as the basic mapping of the samples – defined in the Key Range – you can also use the Parameters area to

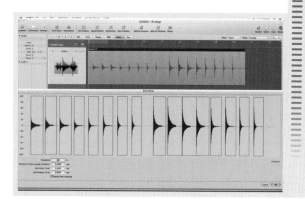

Once you've mastered a couple of auto-mapping options, you may find the process of creating an instrument in the EXS24 Instrument Editor much quicker to achieve. If not, you could choose to manually drag and drop samples directly from the browser onto the corresponding keys.

adjust various playback properties for each zone. For example, you can use the Output options to adjust some rudimentary mixing properties of each zone, setting the respective volume, pan, and – if you instantiated the multi-output version of the EXS24 – the option to route each separate zone to up to 16 individual outputs. This is particularly useful on drum-based instruments because it enables you to route individual parts of the kit – such as the snare, for example – out to separate channels in your Logic mixer, and hence have different EQ, compression and reverb settings.

The Playback parameters have a number of important uses. Both Pitch and 1Shot are especially useful for drum samples. Pitch, once disabled, stops the sample from tracking the keyboard; 1Shot plays the sample for its full duration, irrespective of how long the key is held down for. One of the more creative parameters, though, is the Rvrs (Reverse) option, which is an invaluable sound design tool applied to almost any sample you load into the EXS24.

You can also change some other important properties in how the sample's data is read, including Start and End points, as well as looping. Note that with all these parameters you can open up an assigned audio file in the

Sample Editor window simply by [Ctrl]-clicking under the Sample or Loop parameter columns. The corrective applications of these tools are well documented, but they are also useful for glitch-like effects, either cutting hard into the audio file or creating strange, stuttering loop points within the sample.

Making groups
The process of creating and organising groups has seen some major improvements in Logic Pro 8. Groups can now be assembled in much the same way as a playlist in iTunes: simply select the required zone(s) and drag ▶

Power Tip
Although you might take some time in adjusting the EXS24's front panel settings in relation to the mapping you've created in the EXS24 Instrument Editor, these settings won't actually be stored along with the instrument. To store the panel settings – such as the filter cutoff position, for example, or the envelope positions – along with the mapping information, you will have to go through the process of opening up the Options tab on the EXS24's front panel and selecting Save Settings To Instrument.

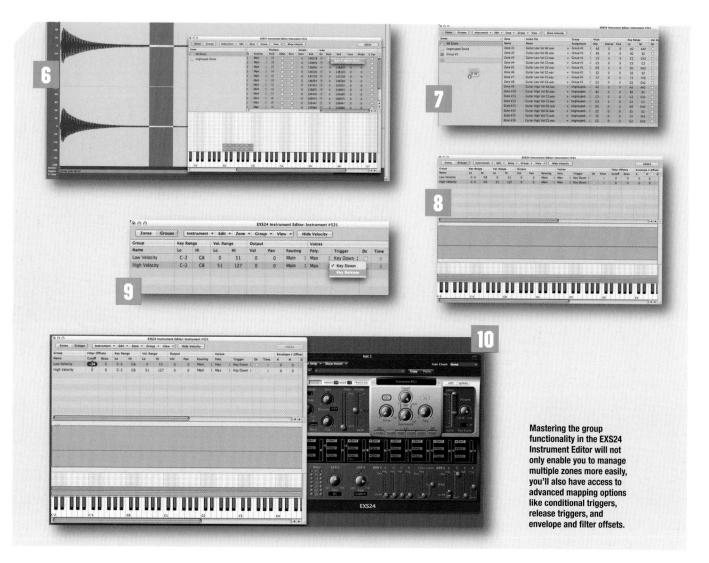

Mastering the group functionality in the EXS24 Instrument Editor will not only enable you to manage multiple zones more easily, you'll also have access to advanced mapping options like conditional triggers, release triggers, and envelope and filter offsets.

THE EDITOR IS JUST AS GOOD AT MANIPULATING THE EXISTING SOUND LIBRARY INTO INTERESTING NEW FORMS.

them over into the Zones column. Note that you can also use the same Zones column to move through the various groups, viewing the zones that relate to that particular group or, in the case of the Ungrouped Zones option, those zones that haven't already been grouped.

As you can see, the groups' functionality is an immediately useful way of organising more complicated zone arrangements. However, moving over to the dedicated Groups view (clicking the button in the top left corner of the EXS24 editor) enables you to access a number of other benefits of groups. One application, for example, is to use the groups to modify and control velocity layers within your instrument. Simply group the 'layers' within your instrument – labelled soft, medium or hard, for example – and use the group's Vel Range control to establish velocity switching between the zones.

Trigger happy
Going further still you can also use groups to create various different triggering options, including release triggering and key switching. Release triggering (using Key Release rather than Key Down in the Trigger column)

enables you to place short audio events after the main note – for reverb tails, for example – or a small, decaying 'resonance' after a piano note is released. Key switching uses 'conditional' MIDI events – such as a Note On command, or modulation wheel movements – to trigger a group. This could be a useful way of moving between different string articulation – such as legato and staccato, for example – simply by toggling two of the lowest keys (C1, D1) on a MIDI keyboard.

Some of the more interesting group controls are the Filter and Envelope offsets. Although you can't have a completely different filter and envelope setting for each zone or group, these offsets do enable you to vary, positively or negatively, the current parameter position on a group-by-group basis. For example, going back to the notion of velocity-switched groups, you could use a filter offset so that a lower velocity group also has a darker filter setting.

Here we've been working on the assumption that you're using the EXS24 Instrument Editor to build a mapping from scratch, but it's important to remember that the Editor is just as good at manipulating the existing Logic sound library into interesting new forms. Whether it's as simple as routing drum sounds through the separate outputs, or copying and pasting layers between different instruments, you'll soon realize that the EXS24 Instrument Editor is the hidden secret in getting the best from this superbly efficient software sampler. MTF

THE CENTRE FOR DIGITAL MUSIC

"We don't just teach how to use today's audio and music technology tools, we teach you how to create the tools of tomorrow!"

- BEng Audio Systems Engineering (3 years)
- MEng Digital Audio and Music Systems Engineering (4 years)

For further information please contact:
Department of Electronic Engineering
Tel: +44 (0)20 7882 5346
email: enquiries@elec.qmul.ac.uk
www.elec.qmul.ac.uk

Queen Mary
University of London

LOGIC PRO 7 WORKSHOP

SPECTRAL GATE

Processing in the spectral domain can lead you to a completely new range of sounds and treatments. **Mark Cousins** finds out what's behind the Spectral Gate.

ogic is packed with many weird and wonderful plug-ins, but none is as utterly perplexing and intriguing as the aptly named Spectral Gate. Is it some kind of advanced processor for cleaning up drum sounds, a means of creating space-age sound effects, or simply a super-charged filter?

In truth, Spectral Gate belongs to a group of plug-ins (which includes Native Instruments' Spektral Delay and iZotope's Spectron) that process sound in the spectral domain. In other words, they split sound into thousands of separate frequency bands and then apply different processes to minute groups of frequencies.

Spectral Gate might not be for the timid, but it does provide a fascinating insight into an entirely different way of processing sound.

To the extreme
The best way to conceptualise Spectral Gate is as an extreme multi-dimensional filtering effect. As such, Spectral Gate is arguably most useful as a means of producing abstract textures that sit behind the rest of a

SPECTRAL GATE PROVIDES A FASCINATING INSIGHT INTO AN ENTIRELY DIFFERENT WAY OF PROCESSING SOUND.

track, the Spectral Gate picking out small clusters of harmonics that are then sent through plenty of additional reverb to complete the effect.

The starting point in this workshop is a simple drum loop – to give the Spectral Gate something to sit against – and an abstract, textural loop culled from another song. Try inserting an instance of Spectral Gate across the Texture Loop track and begin to familiarise yourself with the essential controls and operation of the plug-in. The first element to explore is the relationship between the Threshold, Super Energy and Sub Energy parameters. Like a traditional audio gate, Threshold has a big impact on the resulting effect – in this case, dividing the signal into two components: those harmonics that are above the threshold, and those that are below it. Adjust the Threshold level to hear this in action. **1**

The Super Energy and Sub Energy parameters control the relative level of harmonics above and below the threshold. In most situations you'll want to reduce the relative level of the Sub Energy parameter and leave the Super Energy parameter at its 0dB setting. Try turning

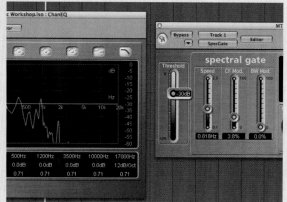

Sub Energy right down (-100dB) and adjusting the Threshold to around -25dB. You should now hear an almost Morse Code-like transformation of the input, with only the highest harmonic peaks slipping through Spectral Gate's filters. **2**

Now turn your attention to the Center Freq and Bandwidth parameters, which sit towards the middle of the plug-in interface. Essentially, the Center Freq and Bandwidth controls add an extra dimension to the filtering effect, so that only the harmonics within a specific frequency range – 200Hz-800Hz, for example – are processed by Spectral Gate. To hear this in action you'll need to reduce the Bandwidth – a level of about 310Hz should make this audible – and tweak the Center Freq control to home in on the group of harmonics you want Spectral Gate to process. This can be a great way of narrowing the effect, putting Spectral Gate's output into a distinct section of the mix. **3**

Another interesting benefit of the Center Freq and Bandwidth parameters is that you can also make use of the Low Level and High Level parameters to bleed in the frequencies on either side of the Spectral Gate. Try increasing the High Level parameter to -20dB or so to hear a high-pass-filtered component of the original input. This is an excellent way of adding sparkle and texture to the otherwise harmonically pure output so often created by Spectral Gate. **4**

Water gate
The effect of Spectral Gating wouldn't be complete without a few additional plug-ins to blend the effect in with the rest of the mix. As we have already mentioned, reverb should be considered an essential complementary effect, especially if Spectral Gate is just outputting a few

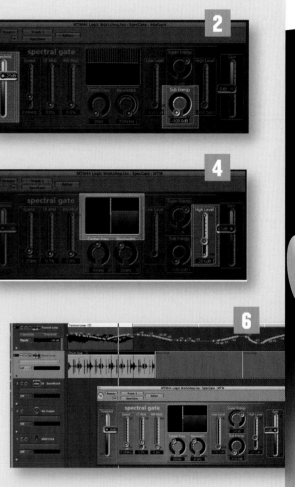

Spectral Gate can produce some marvellous abstract textural treatments. Try using just the Super Energy output combined with some tight filtering – using the Center Freq and Bandwidth parameters – to create a characteristically narrow output.

spectral blips because of a high Threshold setting. If you've got the CPU power to spare, make Space Designer your first choice, set up with a suitably long reverb time – five seconds, for example – and a bias towards a wet, rather than a dry, mix.

Another interesting effect can be achieved simply by placing an instance of BitCrusher before Space Designer. With just a touch of Downsampling – say 7x – BitCrusher can really enhance the bell-like qualities of Spectral Gate's output. **S**

Returning to Spectral Gate, you can add movement to your track courtesy of its LFO section. Speed sets the initial rate of the LFO, while CF Mod and BW Mod set the amount of modulation applied to the Center Freq and Bandwidth controls respectively. The best results come from subtle movements and variations. Try a slow Speed setting – say 0.259Hz – combined with only a discreet amount of CF Mod – say 3%. You can also achieve some interesting results by automating the Threshold parameter, bringing out various qualities of Spectral Gating at different points in the song. **6**

THE REWARDS ARE SOUNDS AND TREATMENTS THAT ARE ALMOST IMPOSSIBLE TO ACHIEVE ELSEWHERE.

Spectral Gate might not be the kind of plug-in you'll turn to on a regular basis, but it is one of the many facets of Logic that can really ignite your imagination. Though it takes a little time to understand the interaction of the Threshold, Super Energy and Sub Energy parameters, the rewards of your efforts are sounds and treatments that are almost impossible to achieve elsewhere.

In a world that is populated by so many similar-sounding EQ, compression and reverb plug-ins, it's always refreshing to find something that is distinctly different from the norm – and that is Spectral Gate, a plug-in that will challenge your perception and understanding of sound processing and of just what can be achieved in the virtual domain. **MTF**

Power Tip

Have you ever written a series of automation moves only to discover that the track, at a later point, needs to be lifted by a few decibels? Rather than rewriting the moves, there are two simple solutions: the first is to insert the Gain plug-in into the channel and increase the level that way; the second is to [Apple]-click on the small bar meter in the tracklist and raise the automation curves up or down as a group.

Danny Byrd

It's been ten years since *Manhattan* and Danny Byrd is still going strong. Once an Atari/Akai stalwart, he has since become fully converted to Logic Pro.

Like so many producers, Danny Byrd started off making tracks on an Atari ST and an Akai sampler. It's probably the most basic setup of all, but also – as history will surely testify – one of the most powerful. Although involved with the D'n'B scene since the late 90s, it wasn't until he teamed up with the now legendary Hospital Records in 2000 that he really stamped his authority on the scene, becoming known as a pioneer of the more soulful and vocal liquid funk sound. He's also made quite a name for himself on the remix circuit, racking up successes with the likes of London Elektricity and High Contrast, and finding support from a whole roster of industry luminaries, spearheaded by the likes of Annie Mac, High Contrast and Bryan G.

Initially a reluctant convert to Logic, it wasn't long before the hardware approach to music-making fell by the wayside and Danny took his productions fully 'inside the box'. And careful sonic weapon selection has kept Danny's sound fresh, up front and in demand. We caught up with him in his studio in the South West.

"I first started using Logic because at the time it was deemed by most producers to be head and shoulders above the competition. And I wanted to use a Mac, so it

seemed the logical choice. I'm glad I did, because I think for me Logic has always smashed the opposition with its instruments. Nothing can beat the ease of use of the EXS [sampler] and its integration within the program, and even the ES2 [soft synth] is still very usable for getting great sounds today."

When Danny's producing he uses Logic for everything. "I don't even have an audio editor, like Peak or Sound Forge. I do it all within Logic. And I'm not really using any hardware any more, so Logic is the studio. I have an identical setup on my laptop for when I am travelling around the world DJ-ing, and I really love the Save Project feature, because I know that every single file relating to the song is being saved within that folder. It's very reassuring!"

"Most tracks start off in Logic with just a few drum hits as audio and a few breaks from Stylus RMX. From there they all get processed through a drum buss with the Ad-Limiter on. Next I'll audition lots of different musical samples via the EXS."

Atari/Akai combination

To begin with, Logic seemed overly complicated as an alternative to his trusty Atari/Akai combination.

"Things like the Environment can take a while to get your head around, but then once you've learned what you need to know there's no turning back. The way Logic changed how I work was quite drastic, as I was making the move from using an Atari to sequence an Akai sampler. It was great to be able to save everything directly onto the hard disk in a second, rather than having to use a stack of floppy discs. I guess Logic has made me go a lot deeper into my arrangements than the Atari ever did – if

> "Logic has made me go a lot deeper into my arrangements than the Atari ever did."
> DANNY BYRD

SELECTED KIT LIST

- Apple iMac and MacBook running Logic Pro
- MOTU Mach 5
- Cakewalk Rapture
- Spectrasonics Stylus RMX
- iZotope plug-ins
- Camel Phat and Space
- Mackie HR824s
- Akai MPCs (various models)
- Yamaha EX-5
- E-mu Proteus 2000

Danny in his studio – Apple iMac taking pride of place running Logic Pro.

"If you were to strip me of all my third-party plug-ins, I wouldn't miss them much." DANNY BYRD

you had 64 tracks playing on the Atari then the whole production process would slow right down, and it was hard work to do even little edits here and there. But of course now, with Logic, it doesn't really slow down at all, so you can just get right into the flow of making music. I've even had some songs running with 150-plus tracks!"

"The best thing about Logic is its completeness out of the box. If you were to strip me of all my third-party plugs, well, I really wouldn't miss them too much as I can get the job done with just the Logic plug-ins. The feature that probably makes Logic hard to understand at first is probably its greatest feature: the ability to tailor the software to your own needs, what with screensets, key commands and so on."

With any producer, speed around the studio – be it real or virtual – is key to producing tracks that sound fresh with an irrepressible energy. Danny's philosophy is to create something that is sonically up there with the competition, but something that's also musically creative and new – "Hopefully, if one of these areas is lacking then the other makes up for it!"

"As for the what's coming up, I've just released my album on Hospital Records – *Supersized* – and I also have a sample pack coming out for Loopmasters with some of my best drum'n'bass production tools in there. I've not

Danny currently uses Logic Pro 7 – this is one of his Drum'n'Bass arrangements.

held anything back with that one; you get access to all my best production sounds. Apart from that I'm keeping busy with lots of remixes, bootlegs and DJ-ing.

Danny's top Logic tips

"Everyone seems to have the floating transport bar, but I always fix mine into the top left corner by selecting it from the View menu – the function named Transport.

I always knew you could save your own channel strips, but an often overlooked feature is that you can copy and paste channel strips – essential for quick auditioning!

If you have, say, ten layers of percussion and drum hits making up one break, select all the parts and add them into a folder. Now you can chop up that folder with the scissors as if it were just one break. Re-arranging the cut parts is very good for vintage jungle-style edits." MTF

Subscriptions
Subscribe to MusicTech Focus

☐ **YES!** I would like to subscribe to MusicTech Focus

☐ UK: £19.95 every 3 issues – save 17%
Please complete the Direct Debit mandate

☐ Europe (inc. Republic of Ireland): £54.95 for 6 issues
☐ Rest of World (inc. USA & Canada): £69.95 for 6 issues
Pay by Sterling cheque or credit/debit card

YOUR DETAILS
Title _____ Initials ____ Surname _____
Address _____
_____
_____
Postcode _____Country _____
Tel no. (inc. STD) _____
Email address _____

PAYMENT METHOD
☐ Sterling cheque (payable to Anthem Publishing Ltd)
☐ Visa ☐ Mastercard ☐ American Express

Card no ☐☐☐☐☐☐☐☐☐☐☐☐☐☐☐☐
Expiry ☐☐☐☐ Signature _____

INSTRUCTION TO YOUR BANK OR BUILDING SOCIETY TO PAY DIRECT DEBIT

Anthem PUBLISHING

Originator's Identification Number: 8 3 7 1 8 1

Send entire form to Freepost RRBS-LRRG-CTBJ, Music Tech Magazine, Anthem Publishing Ltd, 800 Guillat Avenue, Kent Science Park, Sittingbourne ME9 8GU

1 Name and address of your Bank or Building Society
To the Manager _____ Bank/Building Society
Address _____
Postcode _____

2 Name of account holder(s) _____

3 Branch sort code ☐☐ ☐☐ ☐☐

4 Account number ☐☐☐☐☐☐☐☐

5 Instruction to your Bank/Building Society Please pay Anthem Publishing Direct Debits from the account detailed in this instruction subject to the safeguards assured by the Direct Debit Guarantee. I understand that this instruction may remain with Anthem Publishing and if so, details will be passed electronically to my Bank or Building Society.

Signature(s) _____ Date _____

UK readers send this coupon to: Freepost RRBS-LRRG-CTBJ, MusicTech Focus, Anthem Publishing Ltd, 800 Guillat Avenue, Kent Science Park, Sittingbourne ME9 8GU

Overseas readers send this coupon to: MusicTech Focus, 800 Guillat Avenue, Kent Science Park, Sittingbourne ME9 8GU, UK

☐ Please tick here if you DO NOT wish to hear about promotions from Anthem Publishing Ltd.

Closing date 30/9/09   Code **MTFLOGI**

LOGIC PRO 8 WORKSHOP

ULTRABEAT

ON YOUR
MusicTech DVD
Full-sized screenshots
and all the supporting
files you'll need to
follow this tutorial.

With several major improvements made in Logic 8, Ultrabeat becomes one of the most exciting virtual beat-creation tools available today. **Mark Cousins** steps to the rhythm.

You only need to look at the continued popularity of tools like Akai's MPC series, Reason's Re-Drum, or Alesis' ageing SR-16 to realise that the drum machine is still one of the most popular ways of piecing together a rhythm track. Ultrabeat, of course, is Logic's answer to the virtual drum machine, incorporating an array of synthesis and sampling technology optimised for drum sound, as well as its own built-in pattern sequencer. For the new user, though, Ultrabeat's interface can appear unapproachable, leading many users to fall back on tried and tested tools like the EXS24, rather than experience the exciting set of new possibilities offered by Ultrabeat.

In light of the revisions that have taken place with Ultrabeat in Logic Pro 8, we're going take a revised look at this powerful virtual drum machine, exploring techniques that produce exciting results, without getting lost in some of the deeper features it has to offer.

Voices

An Ultrabeat kit is made up of 25 possible 'voices', viewable down the left side of the interface. Each voice, as such, represents a different part of the kit, and by selecting the relevant voice, you can see its collection of synthesis-based parameters in the large central section of the interface, each unique to the drum sound you're trying to create or modify. Uniquely, Ultrabeat features up to three different oscillators per voice, some using conventional synth-like controls – including the Phase Osc, Noise Generator, Physical Modelling, and FM – as well as a sample playback source. As tempting as all the synthesis options are, though, most regular users of Ultrabeat tend to stick with samples as its primary sound

Power Tip

If you're going to be working with hi-hats it's important to make use of the Mute Grouping facility, which causes the closed hi-hat to mute the open hat when it occurs, and vice versa. To create a group, select the required voice and change its group status from Off to one of the eight available groups. Now select the other voice and change its group accordingly. As well as hi-hats, this trick will work well on kick and snare drums when you're using particularly reverberant samples.

source, only really turning to the synthesis tools to enhance sounds as required.

Let's start by loading an instance of Ultrabeat into Logic, selecting the Multi Output version so as to facilitate further processing options later on. Browsing through the presets, look for the Drag & Drop Samples program as part of the 01 Drum Kits bank. This provides a useful initialised starting point for sample-based kits, enabling you to drag and drop individual elements – like the samples provided on the *MTF* DVD, for example – directly from the browser into the sample holder in Oscillator 2. Remember, though, that the samples aren't stored with the Ultrabeat settings, so you'll need to archive them in a safe place, or use the Copy Ultrabeat Samples To Project Folder checkbox under the Assets tab of your project settings to have them saved with your project. **1**

As an alternative means of configuring your drum sounds, you can always use the Import feature to load in zones from other EXS instruments, or indeed, other Ultrabeat presets. Clicking on the Import dialogue will enable you to browse the Plug-in Settings folders for the EXS24 and Ultrabeat respectively. Once selected, the imported kit will appear 'ghosted out' next to the main voice assignments. Now you can drag these voices from the Import column directly onto Ultrabeat's Voices, assigning each component – perhaps from a number of different presets – as you see fit. **2**

Editing and mixing

With the core samples assigned to Ultrabeat's voices, you can now begin some basic editing and mixing of the samples. Double-clicking on the name of each voice will enable you to rename it accordingly, and you can also use the small blue bar to raise and lower the amplitude, or use the Pan control to set the stereo placement for each voice. The most powerful option, though, is to use the Individual Outputs feature, which enables you to route each voice to a separate mixer channel. Assuming that you've loaded the Multiple Output version, you can access the extra outputs by clicking the small plus sign in the mixer page. Try using compression, equalization, delay and reverb to define each part of the kit – all are tools that play an important part in achieving a release-quality drum sound. **3**

For more advanced sound-sculpting you can also turn to some of the synthesis features within Ultrabeat, often twisting the samples way beyond their original sound and musical role. Looking first at the controls in Oscillator 2, try experimenting with the pitch of the sample – you can often achieve some unique results by retuning drum

Power Tip

When you are piecing together your complete song, you might find it easier to deal with a few regions in the Arrange window, rather than having to switch Ultrabeat's patterns via the keyboard. You export a pattern by clicking and dragging on the small icon next to the pattern and placing the region on the Ultrabeat track in the Arrange window. To avoid the pattern being double-triggered, ensure that the sequencer power button is disabled.

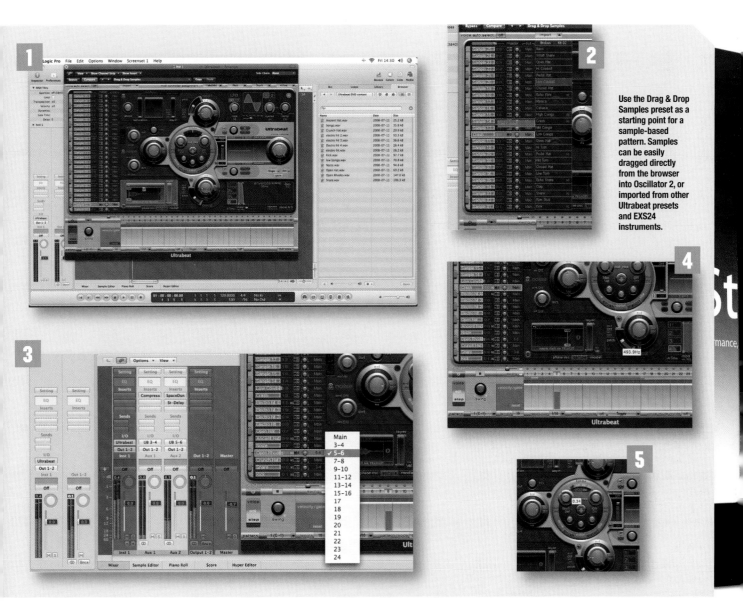

1

2 Use the Drag & Drop Samples preset as a starting point for a sample-based pattern. Samples can be easily dragged directly from the browser into Oscillator 2, or imported from other Ultrabeat presets and EXS24 instruments.

3

4

5

Main
3-4
✓ 5-6
7-8
9-10
11-12
13-14
15-16
17
18
19
20
21
22
23
24

---

samples in an extreme way. The small arrow in the Sample Assignment box can also be used to quickly reverse the sample. This effect can work particularly well on cymbals, possibly using the Sample Start Via Velocity to change the start point within the sample. **4**

Filters and envelopes

Following the Ultrabeat's signal path we can now turn our attentions to the filter, using the four filter modes – low-pass, high-pass, band-pass and band-reject – to tailor the timbre of the sample. For example, you could use the low-pass filter on a kick sample to make it sound deeper, or some band-pass filtering across a snare drum to sit it in a narrower part of the mix. Before you adjust any settings, though, you'll need to ensure that the filter is active by clicking on the Filter legend (when this is lit red, the filter is active). **5**

Embedded into the filter are controls to add distortion to either the filter's input or output. The distortion comes in two varieties: Crush and Distort. Crush offers the grittiest distortion, while the Distort option sounds distinctly more analogue. Both types of distortion sound particularly interesting on kick drum samples, though they can also be useful to add a touch of grit or drive to hi-hats

and snares. If you're using the filter, the routing (defined by the relative orientation of the central arrow) can also have a big effect on the eventual output. For example, try using the filter after the distortion to remove some of the high harmonics added by the overdrive, while at the same time preserving the added body. **6**

Envelopes also offer plenty of creative possibilities for manipulating your drum sounds, either to manipulate the filter cutoff, for example, or to change the sample's amplitude over time. Each voice can have up to four different envelopes, editable from the bottom right corner of the synthesis section. To assign an envelope to a parameter, change the Mod parameter beside the control (in blue writing) to the required envelope generator. **7** ▶

Power Tip

As well as a conventional phase and FM oscillator, Osc1 also features an intriguing sidechain input control. Using the sidechain input enables you to embed any sound in your mix into Ultrabeat's architecture. For example, feed a heavily distorted electric guitar to bus 1 – with the bus and channel fader removed from an output assignment – and then use Osc1 to key gate the guitar in time with the beat, adjusting the envelope to change the relative duration of the gating effect.

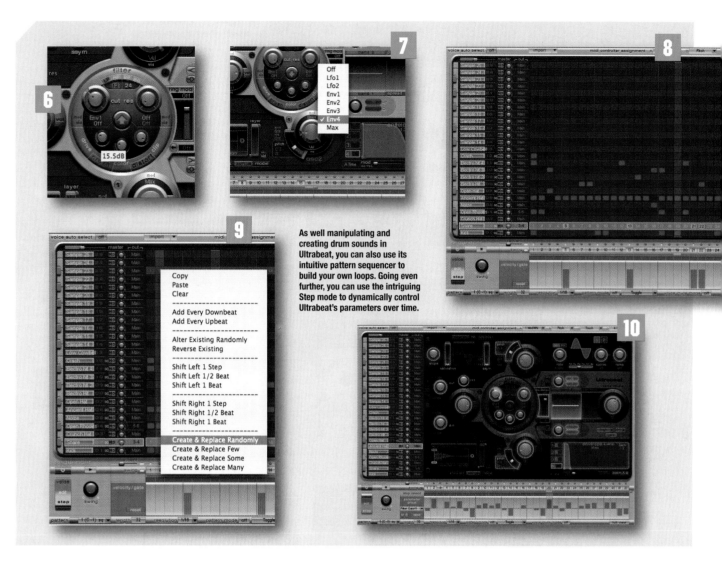

As well manipulating and creating drum sounds in Ultrabeat, you can also use its intuitive pattern sequencer to build your own loops. Going even further, you can use the intriguing Step mode to dynamically control Ultrabeat's parameters over time.

EXPLORING EVEN MORE OF THE SYNTHESIS CONTROLS CAN OPEN UP A HOST OF NEW, EXCITING HYBRID SOUND POSSIBILITIES.

▶ Of course, a virtual drum machine wouldn't be complete without some form of pattern-based sequencer, and in this respect Ultrabeat has plenty of tricks hidden up its sleeve. Each voice has its own Trigger row, where you can input 'step' events with an accompanying velocity and gate time (length, basically) for each step. Pressing the Full View button in the bottom right corner of the interface enables you to see all 25 voices across a grid-like editor, which is a far more conducive way to building up a complete pattern and seeing the interaction between several key voices. A global Accent lane also enables you to program an adjustable accent (using the small slider) over the pattern – emphasising the main downbeats, for example. 8

Exploring the sequencer further highlights some particularly creative features. For example, [Ctrl]-clicking on any trigger row brings up a unique contextual menu that enables you to perform various transformations to the data. Alongside the usual cut, copy and paste tools you'll also find options to, for example, add events on every downbeat, create a new series of random events, or shift the pattern left or right by steps or beats. 9

One of the most powerful sequencer functions, however, is the Step Edit mode, which effectively enables you to store up to 32 step positions for 30 or so key Ultrabeat parameters. The creative possibilities arising from this function are obviously going to be tremendous, but for a start, try creating a pseudo-random resonant filter movement across the hi-hat.

To do this, go out of Full view and change the Edit mode from Voice to Step. You should now see Ultrabeat's interface lit up to indicate which parameters can be 'stepped'. Click and drag on Cutoff to create an initial offset – the parameter offset should change to say Filter Cutoff. Then you can simply draw in the offset for each step on the grid. 10

Beat it!

The scope and potential of Ultrabeat goes far beyond what we've covered here, but at least you'll have some understanding of its key features and how to go about creating your own personalised rhythm tracks. Exploring even more of the synthesis controls – such as the ring modulator, physical modelling, FM oscillators, and so on – can open up a host of new, exciting hybrid sound possibilities, merging the best qualities of both sampling and synthesis to good effect. Even used in its most basic way, though, Ultrabeat will delight and inspire, and certainly offer a new way of looking at the rhythmic qualities of your music. MTF

Power Tip

Changing the relative gate time of a voice sound – especially when you are using samples of a longer duration – can be an interesting way of establishing more groove. You need to make sure the Gate button is active (you'll find it just beneath the large voice volume control) and then you can adjust the gate time, in quantized steps, in the velocity/gate track lane. Try using shorter gate times with lower velocities, and longer gate times on the main beats.

100% CUBASE!

MusicTech Focus

Cubase

The in-depth guide for the creative musician

DVD ROM FREE INSIDE

48 PAGES OF **CUBASE 4** WORKSHOPS

132 PAGES OF PURE CUBASE!

Anthem PUBLISHING

MusicTech Focus: Cubase

ISBN 0-9552170-7-5

£7.99

9 780955 217074

Written and compiled by Music Tech Magazine's Cubase experts

On sale Thursday 27 November, £7.99 with free DVD.
Available at WH Smith (UK), Borders and Barnes & Noble (USA),
and good bookstores in Australia, Canada, Germany and Sweden.
Or order online at www.musictechmag.co.uk/mtm/focus

WHSmith

BARNES & NOBLE
BOOKSELLERS

BORDERS.

LOGIC PRO 8 WORKSHOP

MASTERING IN LOGIC

Mastering may be something you leave to the pros but, with the right technique, good results can be achieved using Logic's bundled processors. **Mo Volans** takes the lead.

Most producers take no chances when it comes to mastering and either employ a professional mastering engineer or have dedicated hardware in their studios for the task – or at the very least a slew of third-party plug-ins. These means of giving your tracks that final spit and polish will often achieve excellent results, but they all have one thing in common: they're expensive.

Many people feel that, after parting with their hard-earned wedge to purchase the latest version of Logic Pro and a shiny new Mac, spending more cash on having their tracks mastered professionally is a step too far. Others may simply not need the level of quality that pro engineers and dedicated hardware can produce. If your music is intended for demo purposes or for club play only, anything beyond a carefully considered DIY job could be seen as overkill.

So you may be pleasantly surprised to learn that, nestled amongst the myriad plug-ins that Logic now ships with, is a collection of virtual devices more than capable of adding that extra edge to your final mix. Plug-ins that you may currently perceive as only useful for mixdown and tracking could become indispensable mastering

WHEN YOU ARE BUILDING UP A SUITE OF PLUG-INS FOR MASTERING, THE ORDER OF THE PROCESSORS IS PARAMOUNT.

tools. For instance, the Linear Phase EQ looks suspiciously like Logic's standard Channel EQ, but what's going on under the bonnet is a different story: a much more processor-intensive algorithm makes this a more suitable tool for mastering. And this is the case with many of Logic 8's improved plug-ins.

Even the Compressor has had a serious overhaul in Logic 8. It now includes vintage modelling, output distortion, a built-in limiter and a handy mix function to enable on-the-fly parallel-compression-style effects. When you add these new features to Logic's dedicated mastering processors, a high-quality mastering chain is just around the corner.

New order

When you are building up a suite of plug-ins for the purpose of mastering, the order of the processors is paramount. For instance, heavy compression can really help iron out a track's dynamics, but it can also reduce

the amount of perceived low frequencies in the audio. Post-dynamic equalization, therefore, is going to be much more effective than using EQ before the compression stage. Lost frequencies can be dialled back in and the compression will appear more transparent.

There are guidelines like this that run right through the process of constructing our mastering chain. However, none of them are strict rules, of course, and once you are familiar with the basics, common sense will prevail. But for now, we'll run through, in order, the processors in a typical mastering setup, so you can get an idea of how Logic's plug-ins can be fully utilised.

On the level

Once the unmastered file is loaded into Logic, one of the first things to think about is the overall dynamic signature. It's fair to say that most of us look to gain as much volume from the mastering process as we can and this really starts with a technique called buss compression, which basically involves strapping a decent-quality compressor across the entire master buss/channel.

The standard compressor supplied with Logic Pro 8 is well-suited to the task of buss compression and has some features in its newly expanded control area that can be extremely useful. ■ For instance, there is an Output Distortion option; when this is used at low settings it can impart a really nice warmth to your overall mix. A Mix function is also supplied, enabling you to re-introduce

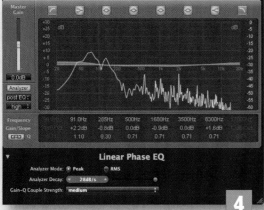

Good dynamics control and equalization in the mastering stage are essential. With Logic 8's new compressor and linear phase EQ, this area of production is well taken care of. Clear metering also helps you keep track of your dynamic content and frequency response.

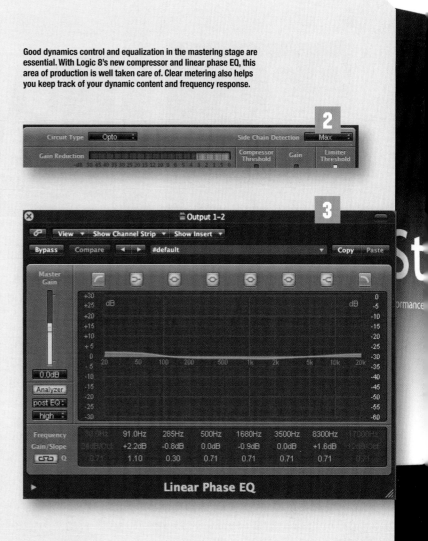

some of the dry, untreated signal back into the mix, essentially creating a parallel compression setup.

When using compressors for controlling the dynamics of a full mix, the aim is to achieve total transparency. In other words, any compression that is applied should have the desired effect but not be audible to the listener. If this is achieved the track will be dynamically uniform throughout, yet will retain all its original character.

This transparency is achieved by using low threshold settings, small ratios and very slow attack and release times. When using these sorts of values you can afford to apply quite generous amounts of gain reduction **2** without introducing any noticeable artefacts.

Broad brush

Once you are happy with the dynamics of your track, you can start to add subtle EQ to enhance or suppress problem areas of the mix. Broad brush strokes are needed here to ensure that no one sound is over-coloured by the effects of the EQ. This further transparency is achieved by using low Q factors and small amounts of gain, and of course, the right equalizer plug-in.

Most standard EQ plug-ins work in quite a destructive

manner, often introducing minimal amounts of phase distortion and delay into a signal. These EQs are very CPU-efficient, creating only small amounts of latency. Due to these qualities, these more generic EQs can be used with great results in a mixing environment, but they are not perfectly suited to the application of mastering.

The ideal EQs for mastering are those that use linear or minimal phase algorithms to process sound. These algorithms do require more number crunching and therefore apply more pressure to your CPU, but it is likely that most systems can handle this extra pressure when you're only working with a few instances of the plug-in on one channel. Any extra latency introduced by these more intensive processors should not be of any significance while you're mastering, as no recording or MIDI is used at this stage.

Power Tip

Most of us want the loudest master possible but there should be some thought behind level boosts. Not only should your tracks be dynamically pleasing to listen to, it is worth giving a thought to possible overloads and distortion. Some playback devices, especially older ones, can actually overload and produce audible clips at 0dB. It's worth setting your output level to -0.1dB to guarantee good translation. The loss of volume will be negligible.

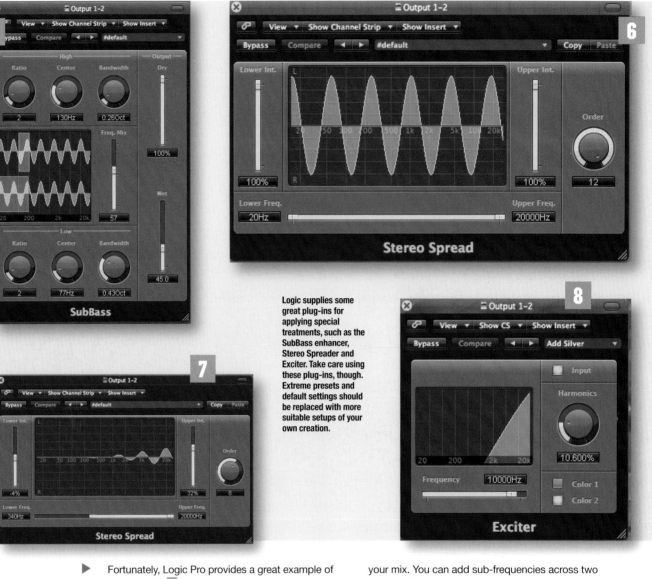

Logic supplies some great plug-ins for applying special treatments, such as the SubBass enhancer, Stereo Spreader and Exciter. Take care using these plug-ins, though. Extreme presets and default settings should be replaced with more suitable setups of your own creation.

▶ Fortunately, Logic Pro provides a great example of linear phase EQ **3** and if you already use the generic channel EQ, the interface will be totally familiar. But even with an EQ as transparent as this, you should only add small amounts of gain at any one point in the frequency range. If you're using lots of low or high end, for example, you need to go back and look at these issues in the mix.

A useful feature of Logic's EQ plug-ins is that they can be used as fully fledged spectrum analysers, the resolution of which is fully adjustable. Simply unfold the newly extended controls and many new options will be available to customise the graphical interface. **4**

Special treatment

Logic offers a whole host of tools for adding extra sparkle to your production. Before we look at the various enhancers it's worth keeping in mind that these plug-ins should be used with a certain amount of discipline. Used in moderation, enhancers can generate pleasing effects, but push them too hard and you can end up with senseless noise. Some mastering engineers even hold the belief that enhancers just add noise to the mix and simply refuse to use them. This is, of course, a subjective opinion and you should let your own ears be the judge.

The first enhancer here is a sub-bass processor, simply named SubBass. **5** SubBass uses psycho-acoustic processing to enhance the lower frequencies of

your mix. You can add sub-frequencies across two separate bands, and these bands can then be mixed together and the overall result added to your dry mix.

This effect can be great when used in electronic music destined for club play and should be used to enhance low frequencies that already reside in your mix. This is not by any means an essential part of the mastering chain and it's advisable to use it only when it's really needed – heavy use of SubBass enhancement on an acoustic folk track may not be ideal!

Next up is Logic's Stereo Spread image enhancer. **6** At first glance you will notice that the default preset can completely destroy your carefully sculpted mix. This is due to the stereo enhancement happening across the board, with no discrimination whatsoever. When you're using this plug-in for mastering, it's essential that the lower frequencies – and possibly the lower mids – are left untouched, otherwise your mix will suffer from intense phase problems and poor translation to mono systems.

Once suitable settings have been dialled into the Stereo Spread plug-in **7** only the upper frequencies should be treated – and these only in small amounts. Used sensibly, however, this sort of enhancement can impart real sheen to your mix.

The last enhancement plug-in in our chain is called the Exciter **8** and it does exactly what you would expect: it excites certain chosen frequencies. This plug-in can work

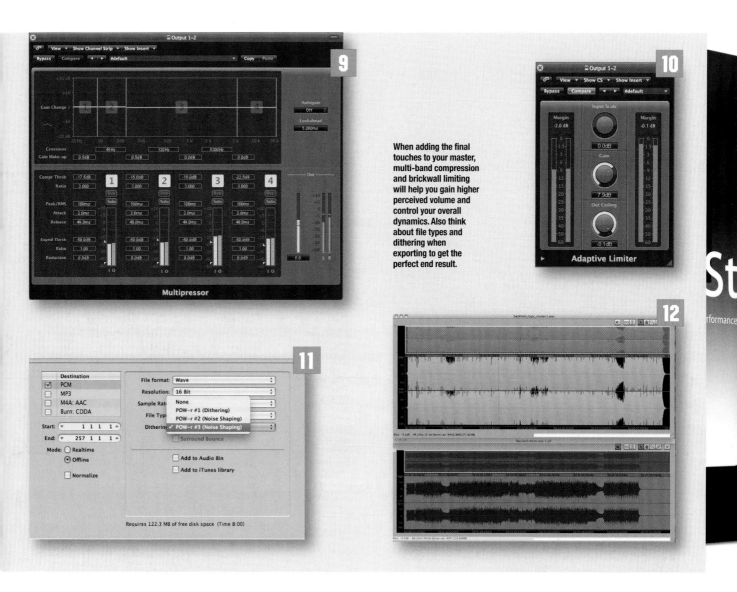

When adding the final touches to your master, multi-band compression and brickwall limiting will help you gain higher perceived volume and control your overall dynamics. Also think about file types and dithering when exporting to get the perfect end result.

across the whole frequency range and can add anything from subtle to very extreme amounts of processing. The Exciter really shines when it's used to enhance very high frequencies. If you stick to the 'less is more' approach, all these enhancement processors can get regular use while you're mastering in Logic.

Final touches

At this stage your master should now be 90% of the way towards being complete and ready for delivery. There are just a few final processes that should take place before you commit your mix to CD or mp3.

One last dynamics check is always a good idea at this stage. All the extra processing added after the single band buss compressor at the start of the chain can introduce extra harmonics and thereby create wayward transients. A good way to deal with these rogue dynamics is to use multi-band compression; this will ensure that problem areas are dealt with and transparency preserved.

A multi-band compressor is essentially a number of compressors, each set to deal with a specific frequency range. This means that if you have a problem residing in your upper-mid frequencies – an uneven vocal or synth part, for example – you can rectify the problem without colouring the rest of the elements in your mix. Logic supplies a fully featured multi-band compressor called Multipressor that is perfectly tailored for mastering. **9**

The final step is to ensure that the master is loud enough and in the correct format for delivery. To attain super-loud volume during mastering, a brickwall limiter must be used as the final processor in the chain. This is basically a limiter that has an input gain control and a user-definable output ceiling. When the input level is increased the audio becomes denser and its perceived volume is increased. Logic's Adaptive Limiter **10** can do a great job of creating loud masters while leaving the dynamic feel of your track pretty much intact.

Making sure you deliver your master in the correct format is, of course, very important. When you finally export your project, Logic will give you a good list of options **11** including file type sample rate and bit depth (remember to use dithering to reduce sample rate to 16-bit for mp3 and CD use) and also whether your export is performed in real time or offline. It's always a good idea to check with your client how they would like the master delivered before completing this final step.

On importing your mastered file into a sample editor it should now be plain to see the effect the processing has had on your material. **12** MTF

Power Tip

Logic Pro 8's revamped Compressor features vintage circuit modelling as standard. This is really useful when it comes to mastering as it enables you to impart extra character to your tracks. The FET and Opto models are especially effective for conjuring up that vintage sound and certainly succeed in achieving the overall feel of analogue hardware. Be sure to experiment with all the new models as some will work better than others on certain tracks.

On your free DVD

To enable you to get the very most out of your copy of *Music Tech Focus Logic Pro* we've included a DVD containing **high-resolution screenshots** from the tutorials, all the necessary Logic session and **audio files for the Workshops** and walkthroughs, plus over **1.5 hours of video tuition** from macProVideo, and demo versions of the very best plug-ins for Logic, including a massive, **800MB demo** of the excellent BFD2.

VIDEO TUITION How to load up and view the 1.5 hours of Logic Pro 8 video tutorials.

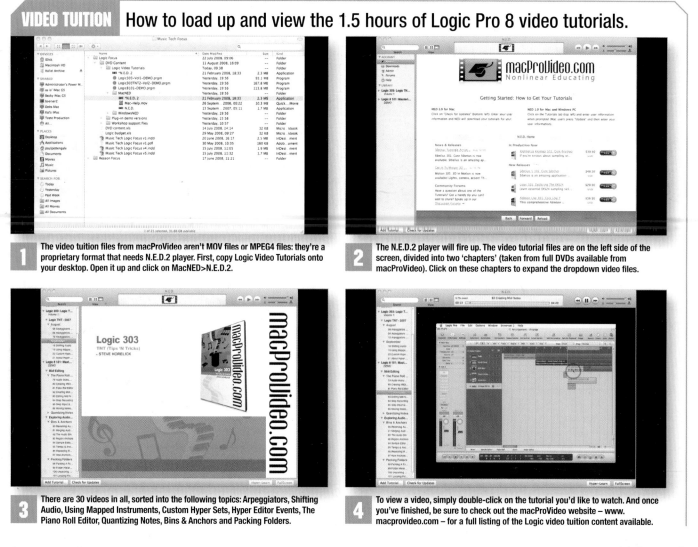

1 The video tuition files from macProVideo aren't MOV files or MPEG4 files: they're a proprietary format that needs N.E.D.2 player. First, copy Logic Video Tutorials onto your desktop. Open it up and click on MacNED>N.E.D.2.

2 The N.E.D.2 player will fire up. The video tutorial files are on the left side of the screen, divided into two 'chapters' (taken from full DVDs available from macProVideo). Click on these chapters to expand the dropdown video files.

3 There are 30 videos in all, sorted into the following topics: Arpeggiators, Shifting Audio, Using Mapped Instruments, Custom Hyper Sets, Hyper Editor Events, The Piano Roll Editor, Quantizing Notes, Bins & Anchors and Packing Folders.

4 To view a video, simply double-click on the tutorial you'd like to watch. And once you've finished, be sure to check out the macProVideo website – www. macprovideo.com – for a full listing of the Logic video tuition content available.